The Conversation of Journalism

THE CONVERSATION OF JOURNALISM

Communication, Community, and News

ROB ANDERSON, ROBERT DARDENNE,
and GEORGE M. KILLENBERG

Foreword by John J. Pauly

Westport, Connecticut
London

Library of Congress Cataloging-in-Publication Data

Anderson, Rob.
   The conversation of journalism : communication, community, and
news / Rob Anderson, Robert Dardenne, and George M. Killenberg ;
foreword by John J. Pauly.
      p. cm.
   Includes bibliographical references and index.
   ISBN 0–275–94448–4 (alk. paper).—ISBN 0–275–95674–1 (pbk.: alk. paper)
   1. Journalism—Social aspects—United States. 2. American
newspapers—Social aspects. I. Dardenne, Robert. II. Killenberg,
George M. III. Title.
PN4888.S6A53   1994
071'.3—dc20   93–40573

British Library Cataloguing in Publication Data is available.

Library of Congress Catalog Card Number: 93–40573
ISBN: 0–275–94448–4
      0–275–95674–1 (pbk.)

First published in 1994

Praeger Publishers, 88 Post Road West, Westport, CT 06881
An imprint of Greenwood Publishing Group, Inc.

Printed in the United States of America

The paper used in this book complies with the
Permanent Paper Standard issued by the National
Information Standards Organization (Z39.48–1984).

10 9 8 7 6 5 4 3 2 1

Copyright Acknowledgment

An earlier version of John Pauly's foreword appeared in *Democracy and Demography
Idea Book*, Vol. 2, published by New Directions for News, Inc., at the University of
Missouri—Columbia, 1991. Used by permission.

Contents

Foreword: Making the News Relevant to Democracy

These are bad days for the American daily newspaper. On every front it imagines itself under assault. One daily after another closes its doors. Readership declines as new competitors, from free suburban weeklies and the yellow pages to CNN and computer billboards, rise up to claim their share of the marketplace. Once-astonishing profit margins dwindle. Public disaffection with the press grows more vocal. Even in journalism education, the tide seemingly has turned. Not so long ago media critic Ben Bagdikian and others complained about all the starry-eyed naifs entering university programs in journalism in the wake of Watergate. Now fewer students each year pursue journalism careers and more seek training in advertising and public relations.

Newspaper owners interpret these facts as evidence of a marketing crisis and seek ways to recapture their audience—by adapting to the tastes of younger readers, appealing to the African-American and Latino middle class, sprucing up their writing, and making their papers more visually stimulating. It will take more than clever marketing to cure journalism's ills, however, as Rob Anderson, Robert Dardenne, and George M. Killenberg persuasively argue. American journalism is suffering from a profound anomie. The concern for the economic condition of newspapers masks a more fundamental unease about the declining cultural authority of the newspaper as an institution, reporting as a profession, and news as a form of knowledge.

Anderson, Dardenne, and Killenberg offer an alternative. They envision the daily newspaper as a common carrier for civic discourse, a medium for conversation among citizens rather than a conduit for professionally packaged information. This suggestion may perplex working journalists. "Isn't that what journalism already does—serve the public interest?" they may ask. "Isn't news already the backbone of democracy, the vital information citizens need to participate in decision making?" The simple answer is, no. There is reason to think that news, as it is currently practiced, is largely irrelevant for democracy.

Before you begin to question how three longtime students and practitioners of journalism could come to such a gloomy conclusion, you should know that, in fact, theirs is a book filled with hope, an extended meditation on the ways in which the daily newspaper might once again engage citizens and, in the process, recapture their loyalty as readers. Anderson, Dardenne, and Killenberg believe the press has a democratic mission, and they suggest innumerable practical strategies by which daily newspapers might reconnect themselves to the communities they serve. To their inspiring chorus, I want to add a slightly gloomier voice, if only to ensure that no one underestimates the task the authors have set before us.

In these days of ephemeral loyalties, journalism's mythic hero remains the Constant Reader—the citizen who devotedly reads the newspaper every day in order to stay informed. At root, this mythic reader may be little more than an occupational psychosis writ large, a defense of the news junkie's addiction as civic virtue. Nonetheless, Americans consistently profess, at least in public, that reading the news makes one a good citizen (and that ignoring the news means one is apathetic). By this view, citizens' assiduous efforts to stay informed guarantee that public opinion remains vigilant and government responsive and accountable. All our protracted debates about journalism—about the form and content of news-papers, the social responsibilities of journalists, the effects of stereotyping and bias, and the consequences of monopoly owner-ship—make sense only if we assume that news is relevant to democracy.

Our utopian hopes for the daily newspaper are actually one instance of a familiar habit of American thought: our tendency to treat the media of mass communication as icons of social order. In a familiar sense, the media call society into existence by creating the infrastructure of everyday life, connecting and coordinating society's parts and investing those connections with meaning. But "the media" are themselves symbols with which Americans habitually think about modernity. The media create a stage upon which modern society plays itself out, but they soon become characters in that drama as well.

Talk about the media, understood in these terms, is always culturally significant. For example, when we complain about children's television viewing—about how much and what they watch—we are making their use of television into a parable of generational conflict. Debates about children's viewing habits are a way of wondering aloud about what the world is coming to or why our children seem alien to us. Similarly, we make fun of grocery store tabloids in order to ridicule (in a socially sanctioned way) the presumably uneducated people who read such papers. Finally, our hand-wringing about the morality of movies recog-nizes the politics of cultural power: we know that those who control the processes of cultural production decide whose way of life will be effaced and whose moral values will be publicly displayed and honored. Talk about "the media," in short, inevitably slides into talk about class, status, power, the nature of urban life, and the consequences of capitalism and industrialization.

What has the daily newspaper signified for Americans? For over a century, it has served as a totem of democracy. Even as the newspaper declines in relation to other media, as advertisers and readers alike turn away, our public rhetoric clings to the hope that the daily newspaper will sustain our political life. We use talk about the newspaper to convince ourselves that we live in a democracy, often despite much evidence to the contrary.

Americans' identification of the daily newspaper with democracy began, in part, as a historical accident. Had the nineteenth-century newspaper faced the same competition from other media as its twentieth-century counterpart, had the United States chosen public ownership of the telegraph and subsequent electronic media, had trade unionists or socialists been able to sustain an independent communication network, Americans might have invested their democratic hopes elsewhere. For better or worse, however, the commercially supported urban daily newspaper had staked its claim to public opinion by the mid-nineteenth century and has never fully relinquished it.

The newspaper secured its place in American political mythology by helping liberalism resolve one of its recurring theoretical dilemmas. By its very nature, liberal political theory offers only a thin account of what holds citizens together. (I am using the terms *conservative* and *liberal* in their traditional and most meaningful sense, to distinguish the defenders of tradition and social hierarchy from the proponents of individual freedom and social change.) European conservatives always assumed that hierarchy was natural, and they derived their political prescriptions from their broader assumptions about human nature and the limits of individual reason. The mass of men and women, conservatives agreed, would never have the time, resources, sophistication, or devotion to become learned participants in public life.

Liberalism, by contrast, urges groups to free themselves from the status quo. For liberals, society is an artifact, as Roberto Ungar has argued in *Social Theory*—a work constantly being remade in the name of freedom and equity rather than a finished product to be cherished and preserved in its original form. In a society committed to the future rather than the past, the sources of solidarity must remain forever elusive. Eighteenth-century philosophers often imagined "civil society"—a domain of relations outside the control of the state—as liberalism's shared social world. Civil society proved anything but liberating, however, for embedded in it were great inequities of literacy, wealth, gender, and race.

Not surprisingly, liberals turned to the newspaper for a model of social order. Weekly newspapers, after all, had helped foment the American Revolution. Until the invention of the telegraph, almost all public information had moved through newspapers that were carried in the mail. This widespread exchange of newspapers, in turn, solved American democracy's problem of scale. Political theorists like Montesquieu had long assumed that a republican state must remain small and local if citizens hoped to control it. The scale of empire, they thought, would corrupt republican virtue. But eighteenth-century American intellectuals proposed to do what Montesquieu had thought impossible: establish a continental democracy by using newspapers and the postal system to draw the country together and allow citizens to monitor the state at a distance. By the mid-nineteenth century, the nation's political fortunes had been indissolubly wed to the newspaper.

The intrinsic properties of the newspaper have made Americans' hopes for it plausible. Its relative cheapness makes it a medium for all citizens, regardless of social class. The use of new technologies such as fast printing presses and the telegraph have often enhanced its democratic aura. Fast presses reduced unit costs and allowed a wider dissemination of information, and the telegraph equalized regional advantages in news access, bringing all sections of the country into instantaneous contact. Even the newspaper's character as a miscellany seemingly put it in the service of democracy. Variety is basically a marketing strategy that helps publishers gather a mass audience for advertisers, but it is also a cultural strategy that simulates the feel of democracy. By printing a wide range of stories, the newspaper offers the common reader encyclopedic knowledge at a cheap price.

Ultimately, the daily newspaper's variety made it an apt symbol of urban life. We now forget that in the mid-nineteenth century the daily newspaper was widely considered a new technology, with a content, scale, form of production, and pace that felt distinctively contemporary. Even today, surrounded by newer media, we continue to think of the daily newspaper as a voice of city life. It symbolizes the frivolity, inattentiveness, incoherence, and reckless pace of the city, yet its inclusiveness symbolizes as well our hopes for a cosmopolitan society. When Anderson, Dardenne, and Killenberg urge the newspaper to become a community forum for a multicultural society, they invoke a long tradition of analysis and concern.

So much for the good news: disappointment over the newspaper's actual performance followed its inception all too soon. As one of the first mass media to simulate society as a whole, the daily newspaper was also one of the first to disenchant Americans. (While the triumphs of recent technologies like the computer are all around us for now, their most hideous failures lie ahead.) By the end of World War I, the inadequacies of the daily newspaper were evident to almost everyone. In his 1922 book, *Public Opinion*, Walter Lippmann relentlessly catalogued the failures of the press during the recent war. By its very nature, news could never provide adequate knowledge for democracy, Lippmann argued. He noted the arbitrariness and bias of news selection, the hurried pace of news work, the indifference of the audience, the imperial prerogatives of ownership, and the inadequate education of journalists.

After the war, reformers would continue to search for ways to make the mass-circulation, advertising-supported daily newspaper a better servant of democracy. Viewed in retrospect over several decades, each reform now looks like a battle in a larger campaign to purify and restore the daily newspaper as a symbol of democracy. Many of these battles were fought in the name of professionalism. Ethics codes, university training in journalism, and quasi-scientific methods were proposed as ways to make news a reliable ally of democracy. There were other strategies, too, though. As the mainstream daily press refashioned itself into an objective, fact-gathering enterprise, it banished literature from its pages. Journalists stigmatized public relations and advertising professionals, on whose work they so heavily relied, in order to dramatize the comparative dignity of their own occupation. And publishers condemned the new broadcast technologies as purveyors of mere entertainment rather than information.

In envisioning a news-based democracy, Americans conceived the first version of what we have come to call an information society—a social order organized around the marketing of industrially manufactured cultural commodities. Anderson, Dardenne, and Killenberg argue that a social order imagined in these terms can never be genuinely democratic. A newspaper that is committed to "covering" reality every day has no time to listen to its citizens. A business office that tries to define readers as a market will never understand them on their own terms. A medium that invests so much in gathering information may not interpret that information with equal care. Reporters who treat research as a bureaucratic routine will habitually gloss local culture.

The authors speak often and eloquently of the failures of much contemporary journalism. Let me only add a summary of my own objections to the concept of a news-based democracy. I wish to affirm many of the same hopes for the daily newspaper held by Anderson, Dardenne, and Killenberg, but I also wish to discover in the failures of the daily newspaper a cautionary tale about the ways in which any vision of an information society will inevitably betray our hopes for democracy.

There are four reasons why I think a society organized around the principle of information can never be democratic. First, an information society invests too much faith in technologies of communication rather than in the social commons. As a technology-driven metaphor for the communication process, the term *information* constantly mistakes technical improvements, such as decreases in signaling time or increases in channel capacity, for improvements in communication. Whenever we allow the rhetoric of information too central a place in our discussions, we substitute technical for political considerations and encourage forms of communication that preempt democratic governance. Technologies that emphasize speed of transmission and control of space will always create a dilemma for democratic theory, for they tend to foreclose the possibilities of local ownership and control.

Second, an information society imagines citizenship in overly individualistic terms by identifying personal satisfaction as a goal best achieved through technological innovation. Curiously enough, both conservatives and radicals find fault with this consumerist account of social order. Conservatives think consumerism undermines civic virtue and self-restraint; radicals think that it undermines social solidarity. Democracy probably wants for both civic virtue and solidarity, for self-restraint as well as mutual aid. An information society tends to undermine social solidarity by creating an ever-expanding market for cultural commodities tailored to individual tastes.

Third, an information society, in the long run, is not physically sustainable. If we listen past the fulsome, clanging praise, we will hear a soft voice whispering that the information society brings social overload and individual neurosis in its wake. Our ever-more elaborate systems for cataloguing and accessing information can never keep up with the sheer volume of data being manufactured. Unable to digest the information we produce, we experience "information anxiety." Much of what we decry today as apathy may, in fact, be a quite human (and political) response to the ever-increasing demands to stay informed.

Fourth, the term *information* badly misrepresents the actual social practices of democracy. If we ponder those social groups in which we have felt democratically empowered and connected, we will realize that information has played, at best, a marginal role in any of them. We cannot profitably use the term *information* to explain why, in different times and places, labor unions, women's groups, local political parties, community organizations, university faculties, and church congregations have felt democratic to significant numbers of citizens, or why banks, factories, the U.S. Senate, the United Nations Security Council, high schools, welfare offices, and, yes, newsrooms have not.

What holds democracy together is not information but a mutual commitment to shared and appropriate ways of knowing. The spirit of inclusion, a respect for evidence, a willingness to give an account of one's reasons in uncoerced conversation, the sense of a shared history—these are some of democracy's enduring virtues. None can be guaranteed, or even adequately described, in terms of information alone.

Anderson, Dardenne, and Killenberg realize that the newspaper cannot do the work of democracy if it assumes that the public is already out there, waiting to be captured in a marketing profile. The public is always constituted, called into existence in and through the newspaper's reporting practices. To help readers cultivate the right habits of mind and heart, the newspaper must address them as citizens.

Journalists might start by reinventing their work as a democratic activity. Journalism needs to be understood as something more than an industry or a profession. As an industry, it is little more than a value-added business—buying newsprint, adding information to attract readers, and then selling those readers at a premium to advertisers. As a profession, journalism is too often the practice of a smug style of expert knowingness. It could offer, instead, a craft for democracy by encouraging ideal practices that all citizens might usefully emulate—an ability to investigate the world, a willingness to test one's assumptions against experience, and the skill to question others, write clearly for one's fellow citizens, and engage in civil disagreement. Those are skills that all citizens need to learn. Journalism, conceived of as a social practice rather than an industry or profession, might thus serve as one model of responsible citizenship.

Journalists will also need to imagine their audiences differently. Adapting to new audiences will mean little if newspapers continue to treat readers as mere consumers of information. Nor will hiring more reporters and editors from underrepresented groups make much difference (however worthy their employment may be as a matter of simple justice) if those new employees are compromised by the existing bureaucratic routines of the newsroom. As Anderson, Dardenne, and Killenberg argue, newspapers need to imagine readers as participants in an ongoing conversation. Journalists themselves, if the truth be known, yearn for a stronger sense of connection with their audience. If the audience remains silent, it may be in part because the newspaper fails to make itself available as a true common carrier of public opinion.

Finally, in one of their book's most striking arguments, Anderson, Dardenne, and Killenberg suggest that journalism needs to listen more and speak less. In particular, it needs to respect the silence out of which democratic culture might grow. At first blush, this argument seems counterintuitive. Silence is in general disrepute among us. We rarely understand it as anything more than an absence. Silence is a shameful refusal to speak out, a condition of subservience and powerlessness, a gap in news coverage, apathy, an opportunity for commercial exploitation, an uncomfortable lull in the conversation, or the bastard child of secrecy. Here is yet another instance of the modern tendency to use the mass media as metaphors for politics and society. The entire liberal tradition praises the value of speaking out and imagines new technologies of communication as a means to extend speech, making information more widely available, and offering new venues for public discourse. Because we think that verbal performances constitute society, silence (by comparison) remains the empty stage to be filled by our spoken lives.

Yet there are forms of silence that we might wish to consider politically virtuous. A democratic society could choose to protect freely chosen silence as vigorously as it does freely chosen expression. Citizens might start by refusing to participate in marketing research that frames their views in standardized language. We might further identify the arts of silence appropriate for a democracy. Tolerance of others is one such art, as is the patience to listen carefully to another's argument. A democracy probably needs to set limits on some new communication technologies in the interests of solidarity and equity. The oral traditions so important to democracy can flourish only with some guarantees of institutional silence. Following this rule, democracies might choose to protect some times and places against incursions of information. Outdoor advertising, telemarketing, television advertising for children, television ads and prerecorded music at sporting events, and the use of commercial newspapers and television in classrooms have all, at one time or another, infringed on spaces and times once given over to silence.

In the end, journalism needs to offer democracy more meaning and less information. As matters stand, journalism contributes far too much to the frenetic pace of everyday life. It could help citizens create a world subject to democratic control, a society of humane pace and scale. To do so, as Anderson, Dardenne, and Killenberg recommend, journalists may need to relinquish their more grandiose professional aspirations and simply open the pages of the daily newspaper to citizens' voices and concerns. If such practices help inspire democracy, so be it.

Let the wild rumpus begin.

John J. Pauly
Saint Louis University

Introduction

"Time's Readers to Talk Back, on Computer" announced a headline in the *New York Times* (Carmondy, 1993). That same day, *USA Today* quoted *Time's* assistant managing editor, Walter Isaacson: "It's nice to create a sense of community in which the magazine is simply not handed down on engraved tablets but instead allows comments, conversations and feedback." Even on a slow news day, Isaacson's words received scant notice, but we found what he said remarkable. Without knowing it, Isaacson summarized and endorsed the message of this book on the very day that we were putting the finishing touches on the manuscript.

The Conversation of Journalism approaches its subject hopefully but critically; we expect that many of our evaluations will be controversial and perhaps rejected as naive or idealistic. But Isaacson, speaking on behalf of an important institution of journalism, seems in harmony with our philosophy and practice.

Time and many other news organizations are coming to grips with journalism as the communication profession it once was and can again become in our electronically linked future. Communication, conversation, and community are the keys, as Isaacson has helped us say.

Despite the outlook evident in *Time*'s plans, many contemporary discussions of the future of journalism—indeed, many strategies now being implemented—remain framed by a false dichotomy: the comparison of information values with entertainment values. The questions implied by this distinction lead the profession in certain directions and highlight certain issues over others. Seen in this light, journalism faces such questions as: Should news organizations include more—or less—serious content and "straight news" when the public seems to want more entertainment? Should newspapers, if they are to survive, become more specialized in addressing specialized audiences, like magazines, or more visually exciting, like television? Should television, given its access to mass audiences, use its power to educate more and entertain less? How much is journalism to blame for the declining quality of public discourse, and how much is this problem the fault of a public that loves complicated soap operas but refuses to try to analyze complicated social and political issues?

Although these are among the relevant and interesting questions that should be addressed in the current media culture, this volume will attempt to accomplish a somewhat different task. We would like to show that journalism, especially in the United States, should neither be bound nor defined by this information-entertainment dichotomy. The primary role of journalism should not be either to inform or to entertain. *The prime role of journalism in our view, and the only way by which it can survive as a viable institution in the public arena, is to take the responsibility to stimulate public dialogue on issues of common concern to a democratic public.* It must, in other words, become a forum for ongoing argument. At some times, providing more and better information will be its tactic for doing so, while at others, entertainment will be the road to such a goal. Often, both information and entertainment will fuel the news. But to imply that journalism faces a choice of information versus entertainment not only oversimplifies our problems, it shackles journalism to an antiquated conception of communication.

A variety of critics have bemoaned the decline of contemporary public discourse. However, in our view, their analyses usually have resulted in blame for someone or something rather than the development of constructive and practical alternatives to address the problem. Interestingly, this may be an artifact of the entertainment culture itself—we expect to be able to identify the villain, to demonize and attack an enemy, if only symbolically. Thus, to some critics, television is the villain, while to others, the villain is an amorphous enemy called "the media" that seems to include everything and everyone from "Hard Copy" to the *Christian Science Monitor* to *Rolling Stone*. At times, politicians are blamed, or lawyers, or perhaps the Wall Street entrepreneurs with their bottom-line, dollar-driven mentality.

Although there is enough blame to go around, we do not think it useful to attack. We have enough faith in the tradition of American journalism to believe that some directions for the future can be found in the practices of the past. However, journalism probably will not be able to maintain its current preoccupation with narrow definitions of detachment, news "coverage," complete objectivity, and market-oriented decision making if it is to take on a rejuvenated role in the democratic dialogue.

We see no other institutions that are as qualified or as prepared as journalism to help people talk about the political, social, environmental, and personal choices they face in an increasingly technological world. What is deficient is not the information needed by the public to vote, make plans for civic improvements, or decide on the merits of school referenda. If anything, journalism has provided information overchoice—access to more information than most citizens can even process. What we need is more motivation and opportunity for readers to become more of a public—that is, for citizens to converse, discuss, argue, and engage each other in a dialogue of comparisons and futures. Although what we term the *conduit function* of relaying information is well established, journalism can, and must, do much more to provide an interactive forum in which the relative quality of competing public ideas may be tested. It is this deceptively simple and direct suggestion that we explore throughout this volume.

We acknowledge the efforts of many news organizations that have worked hard to bring more people and perspectives into the news and to connect more consistently with their various communities. Thumbing through virtually any trade publication reveals examples of newspapers coming to terms with new community relationships. Community-building, conversation-based approaches, a respect for diversity, giving public voice to multiple audiences, and other notions of a journalism of invitation do not merely constitute a fad that will fade in better economic times. Because evidence already points in this direction, we are convinced that the argument we offer is neither completely original nor terribly radical in its implications. Nonetheless, we feel it may serve as a fresh articulation of assumptions—philosophical and pragmatic—that could guide a more conversational journalism.

Each of the three of us, as authors and professionals in communication, has reached similar conclusions from different directions and even different careers. The book reflects our personal dialogue on issues of common concern, but to some extent it also is the result of not always agreeing—at least initially—on professional goals and strategies. Although we have decided to write in a single voice in order to present ideas more directly and engagingly, that voice is the outcome of many reconciled differences of opinion. Yet we agreed on so much that we wanted to contribute to the introspective journalistic conversation that occurs in university offices, corridors, and classrooms and that just as frequently takes over newsrooms as well: the attempt to understand "what journalism is really about." The discussions of academic and professional journalists should spill over more often into each other's territories, and we hope our efforts here will promote this kind of dialogue.

Two of us (RD and GMK) have worked as journalists, and all three of us have been engaged for years in teaching communication skills and theory to university students as well. We appreciate journalism and the news, enjoy being with journalists, and are fascinated by newspapers (which explains our emphasis on the press as the prototypical case of journalism). Not only do we want to see newspapers survive, we want to see them prosper. Like so many people, we look forward to the feel of the paper; we enjoy turning pages from one surprise to the next and get very comfortable in our reading routines. But even from this vantage point, we cannot disagree with many people who find much in the paper to be uninteresting and irrelevant to their lives. Consequently, we want to encourage journalists and teachers to argue more productively about ways to make newspapers and the rest of journalism more involving and relevant.

Scholars from John Dewey through contemporary critics like James Carey and Jay Rosen have discussed the importance of community to news organizations. We have certainly been influenced by their wisdom and acknowledge their contributions. However, our interest in a conversational journalism came not from scholarly sources, but from our practical experience in helping journalism students learn the interpersonal sensitivity that can energize the mechanics of reporting. Since the mid-1970s, two of us (RA and GMK) have collaborated on publications and presentations that explore the potential for dialogue in journalistic practice. It was over coffee at a spring 1991 meeting of the International Listening Association that we solidified the central aim of the book. This friendship, which merged the viewpoint of a committed journalist from a family immersed in the newspaper business with the perspective of a confirmed "media watcher" and communication theorist, created our critique-and-preserve approach: journalism should be scrutinized and criticized constantly because we love it and because its vitality is absolutely crucial to any democracy. Its strengths must, therefore, be identified and protected just as vigorously as its weaknesses are criticized. More recently, a narrative, audience-involving approach to news (a special expertise of RD) has reemerged to contribute to a journalism concerned with public dialogue. From a narrative perspective, critics can view journalism both in its long-range historical dimension, recalling when American journalism was basically narrative in tone, and in terms of its immediate challenges for the waning years of the twentieth century.

One similarity among journalism critiques, including those suggesting bold innovations, is that their authors forget. It does not take many pages into *Civilizing Voices* by Marion Tuttle Marzolf (1991) or *Killing the Messenger: 100 Years of Media Criticism*, edited by Tom Goldstein (1989), to realize that much of the contemporary dissatisfaction with journalism has been expressed before. We will not call out the trumpets for all the suggestions in this book because we know that many good people before us have come up with similar notions.

Part of the curious nature of conversation is that no one statement can ever be isolated as the defining contribution, a nugget of meaning after which no further comment is necessary. A single conversation, like a profession, must be understood inasmuch as possible as a whole, in its forward-moving flow and context. In this same way, our ideas in one book are not intended to be definitive but rather to contribute tentatively to whatever develops from them in the minds and actions of readers. Similarly, when readers come to see the news as part of a continuing conversation, they do not expect every article to be definitive and instead begin to use them for what they are worth—as information about what the community is doing, about what people in the community have to say about it, and as stimulants for considering what they would like to see changed or strengthened in society. A journalism that emphasizes this goal of *assisting talk* is not just performing an informational or entertainment function, it is serving a provocative one as well.

Unless they have been alienated by being neglected or silenced for too long, people want to be included in the deliberations of society. We are convinced of that. But we know, too, that within the profession, the concept of a conversational journalism may be foreign or misunderstood. At the *San Jose Mercury*, one of the nation's on-line newspapers, readers can access stories and discuss them with reporters and editors through the paper's electronic bulletin board. In a recent *Wall Street Journal* article, Walter S. Mossberg (1993) wrote about the *Mercury* and described how one reader questioned a story about San Jose's improved garbage pickup service, noting that his own garbage can sat on the curb for days. The editor responded, thanking the reader for his comments and observing that interactions of this kind can make a newspaper better. Mossberg seemed at least interested in such interaction, but he expressed a reservation that seems common in journalism: "I . . . wondered—forgive my professional parochialism—how the editors and columnists had time to participate in the bulletin boards and still get their work done" (p. B1).

The Conversation of Journalism argues that interacting with people in this manner—with or without the computer links—is part of the work of journalists and that when they stimulate public conversation about the news, they *are* working. So is the system of news in a democratic society.

1

Reconsidering Journalism: News within a Democratic Dialogue

In the 1990s, stories and critiques categorized venerable institutions such as the *New York Times*, *Newsweek*, and the CBS evening news as "old news"—dated, irrelevant, and out of touch. Some observers of the media scene found the purveyors of "new news"—a kaleidoscope encompassing talk radio, MTV, *Mondo 2000*, rap lyrics, the *Village Voice*, and movies such as *JFK*—as hot, passionate, and on target (Katz, 1992). Long before these latest dire reports on the aging, listless mainstream media had even surfaced, news executives, prompted by years of flat-line circulation, slipping ratings, and flagging public confidence, devised strategies to entice a fast-track, consumer-oriented generation that appeared, at least, to have little time to dawdle over the news and scant interest in public life. News consultants emphasized demographically driven graphics, visuals, and news packages. Knight-Ridder experimented by trying out a "Boomer"-aimed paper in Boca Raton, Florida.

Despite substantial efforts to improve its "product" and repair its image, mainstream journalism remains a target of criticism riddled from all directions, including the upwardly mobile, young professionals it courts so arduously. In 1993, a *Los Angeles Times–*

conducted survey (Shaw, 1993) reinforced what news executives already suspected: public attitudes toward mainstream news media continue to range from distrust to disdain. Moreover, adding insult to injury, alternative channels of entertainment news and commentary now enjoy the fruits of a relatively appreciative, engaged public. Even journalism's predominance in political coverage waned in the 1992 elections, when candidates often circumvented conventional news outlets to hit the talk show circuit.

Mainstream journalism's answer to its malaise has been like a health-spa makeover—a facial for a youthful look; a diet of leaner, trendier news; an introspective examination to get "in touch" with "self" and environment. While not without benefit, such superficial treatment leaves the core problem unaddressed: how does journalism reestablish its sense of purpose and worth? The answer, apparently, is not in quick-fix tactics to boost circulation, ratings, and public opinion polls. Like the self-pitying person whose counselor wisely says, "Forget about compulsive self-improvements and help others for a change," journalism might consider concentrating less on itself and more on its relationship to the maintenance of democratic dialogue. Journalism can turn from transmitting news and information to an active role of assisted people-to-people communication that ranges far beyond the printed page or newscast script. Even considering the perceived battle of "old news" versus "new news," mainstream journalism stands alone as the most inclusive, responsible, and committed forum for public discourse. What it needs, evidently, is not to radicalize but to revise in a way that takes advantage of the present yet recalls some of the strengths of an earlier, community-based, and narrative mission in which journalism fueled public talk.

The Conversation of Journalism explores journalism as a *communication* discipline. Until recently, journalism emphasized good reporting and writing, without a comparable consideration of its roles and responsibilities within the far broader context of communication. Changes in attitude and technique have become evident as some journalists have discovered—or, perhaps, rediscovered—the benefits of conversation as both metaphor and practical philosophy. However, unless journalism greatly expands its concept of communication, the profession risks further erosion of its influence and place in society's conversation. Mainstream media no longer dominate the flow of news and information. In fact, increasing numbers of people are seizing the initiative to gather news and information personally, using new media channels of communication to talk with politicians, institutions, each other—and, occasionally, even with those journalists who are especially accessible to feedback. Journalism, we believe, can find success and direction through reconsidering three touchstones: *news*, *communication*, and *community*.

NEWS

Journalism's communication problems begin at the heart of the enterprise—the reporting of news. Conventional news—stories of subjects like urban violence, political corruption, the national debt, and global famine—depresses people because it is so often devoid of hope or promise of improvement. Ironically, some of journalism's best writing and reporting, moving and gripping though it may be, only intensifies the glum perceptions of society. To compound the problem, that staple of mainstream journalism— public affairs reporting—frequently concentrates on colorless, humorless "officials," "spokespersons," and "sources," whose statements are translated and packaged by reporters who strain to write objective accounts of straight news. These accounts seek to present events accurately, but at times, lacking adequate follow-up or context, they curtail or preempt a thorough public discussion of the issues.

When journalism mobilizes on "breaking news" stories, rushing to cover the latest human or natural eruption, a myopic press sometimes forgets to include adequate history and perspective. Given today's computer, telephone, and information technologies, people are flooded with information, with very little of it in a meaningful context. The movement toward more raw information and fewer gatekeepers increases the need for context, interpretation, and analysis. People need to know where information fits in and how it affects them. Does it portend disaster—or something less apocalyptic? Does the latest crisis at the United Nations—or City Hall—involve a mountain of problems or only a molehill? And what can be done? The news frequently leaves people not only bummed out but left out as well.

Even in its important watchdog role, journalism undermines its own credibility by feeding the public's distrust of institutions and leaders through its "gotcha"-style reporting of scandals and malfeasance. Not surprisingly, people have grown increasingly skeptical about the country's condition and fate, and the messengers of depressing, negative news receive a share of the public's blame. Journalists must not ignore bad news, including scandal and malfeasance, but they can expand their definitions of news to include a broader range of what happens to people. It is not only scandal and malfeasance. People are often as hopeful as they are pessimistic, yet journalists find it difficult to report the daily ways in which regular citizens cooperate to build their lives in community. Let's face it, such reporting simply is not as sexy—or as salable.

Journalism, however, misplaces its energy and abandons its central role in the maintenance of democratic dialogue when it attempts to address its problems by better marketing. While certain stories, including juicy scandals, have "audience appeal," they should not crowd out media discourse that generates public conversation which is more central to our lives and well-being. In other words, with our wide-ranging media options, do we really need a newspaper that puts more effort into a weekend entertainment guide than a voters' guide or a TV station that assigns higher priority to a sitcom rerun than to live coverage of a town meeting? Voters' guides and town meetings are not "entertaining" in the same way as weekend sections and sitcoms, but neither are they necessarily boring. They can be interesting and provocative while contributing to public dialogue, provided journalism decides to focus on the excitement of communication rather than the marketability of information.

As a business, journalism requires audiences. But journalism is more than a business. It is a social necessity and a constitutionally protected right; it is one of the major ways in which people come to know and understand their worlds and, therefore, themselves. As such, it requires alert, responsible citizens. Supplying a product for consumers is substantially different than sharing communication with the public. When defined as a stimulus for conversation, news brings people closer to issues and to each other, while it brings people and their lives closer to journalism and journalists.

Journalism tries to suppress its humanness even while it over-markets its so-called "human interest" news. Journalists often transmit facts and information to people they hardly know, using forms and styles that have evolved over the decades into a rigid sameness. These forms and styles—and, therefore, journalists themselves—reflect little individuality or personality, little compassion or warmth. Journalism is an imperfect human creation, yet it lacks the qualities normally associated with a human creation, in part because it hides its own humanity behind such facades as the inverted pyramid, objectivity, truth, fact, official sources, and the cold, hard commercial transaction of a news commodity peddled to consumers.

When journalism exhibits its human side, the image is not always flattering. News delivered with sneers or sarcasm is offensive and reinforces the image of journalists as an effete elite—as supercilious, condescending know-it-alls. It is somewhat like the feeling many people get watching print journalists on the weekend news talk shows—the one phrase no one ever seems to use is, "I don't know."

Journalists can admit their limitations and approach news, not as their exclusive domain, but as a cocreative activity that depends on participation by citizens in the community. Journalists create the news, but they hardly do it alone; they do it in a cultural environment that is itself created by diverse groups. *Journalism is not a communication profession simply because it is communicating news; it is a communication profession primarily by communicating well to cocreate news in the first place.* News is one of the activities through which people strive to make sense out of their lives and the world around them. All people are part of the news because they are part of their culture and because news is a participative narrative that defines the culture in all its diversity. News is not what we receive; it is the culture's story, which develops as it is told. However, conventional journalism often appears to separate people from news rather than integrate them into it. This artificial separation of people from news leads to stilted, contrived, and lifeless accounts that seem to disengage people from their own communities.

Bringing together people and journalism will not happen overnight, nor is it a magic cure for our ills. Nonetheless, alert and cooperative journalists, using narrative and other invitational styles and forms, can interest and engage people in ways that recognize the public's intuitive, pragmatic intelligence. An infusion of broader participation into our news can lead to a more honest, forthright, and understanding journalism—one with a personality and a soul—and one that requires an irrevocable commitment to communication.

COMMUNICATION

Journalists as communicators cannot function merely as objective transmitters of information. They also must be effective listeners and conversationalists, sharing ideas with a public that is clearly more perceptive, socially responsible, and potentially vocal than their profession sometimes assumes. News is a cooperative activity that is constructed and evolves through the conversations of a community.

It used to be that public land available for all to use was called a commons (Snyder, 1990). It was a meeting place where people talked, relaxed, and debated policies. In a sense, journalistic news is such a meeting place, the electronic society's commons and the middle, *public* ground from which people can learn, mature, agree, and disagree—and from which social change can grow. News is not—or should not be—for sale or for anyone's exclusive use, nor should anyone be systematically excluded, for one of the strengths of a commons is its diversity of perspective and opportunity for access.

A recognition of journalism as the new informational commons would substantially differ from the managerial philosophy adopted by editors and managers who wholesale news as a tangible product. They gather information, package it into digestible bits, and convey it to consumers, who themselves have been segmented, targeted, and "sold" to advertisers according to their buying habits. The imagery of commerce is rife in journalism as huge media corporations cooperate with big business to toe the bottom line. News must be more than the currency that circulates through a commercial society. However, such metaphors are reinforced in schools, where journalism students are often taught from linear transfer models of communication: "sources" create "messages" and "transmit" them through "channels" (media) with minimum "noise" (interference) to "receivers." Mass communication is presented as a mechanism—a delivery system with disparate parts, each of which can be tinkered with something like the engine of an automobile.

As news pages fill with theme sections, features, listings, and the other things that editors and publishers think consumers want, the information that people *need* in order to be communicators within the community gets squeezed into smaller and smaller spaces. The more papers attempt to make news items shorter and more accessible, sometimes stripping all but the most exciting facts, the more life they remove from them and, therefore, the easier they make it for people to disengage and distance themselves from the news (and, perhaps, their own communities). People are not passive readers and viewers who ultimately prefer empty entertainment over a news that serves them as citizen-communicators, but they have been invited—in part, by journalism itself—to assume just such a passive role.

We speak here of a conversational *ideal* more than a reality. After all, in an incredibly mobile society, people move every six or seven years, repeatedly change jobs and even careers, and daily subject themselves to thousands of mass-produced ideas and manufactured images. Modern media can create a "homeless mind," in that people can be taken anywhere by news accounts yet feel as though they truly exist nowhere (Berger, Berger, & Kellner, 1974). People lack a "sense of place" (Meyrowitz, 1985), keeping doors closed and radios, TVs, VCRs, and stereos on. They wrap themselves in intricate layers of a media cocoon, knowing all the latest songs and movies, and even much about events across the globe, yet often having no clue about who lives two doors down, or even next door. Sometimes, settled comfortably in their media nests, they avoid opportunities for human contact and communication.

Still, people seem eventually to gravitate to other people. Even those with on-line computers seem to gravitate toward electronic bulletin boards, forums, salons—all services built on human contact and offering opportunities to share ideas, feelings, and skills. Moreover, people still tell stories, participate vicariously in them, and listen for clues to their own lives in the stories of others. Indeed, contemporary social theory is beginning to uncover the power of stories in shaping the central character of social existence (Bruner, 1986, 1990; Coles, 1989; Fisher, 1987). How has journalism responded?

Newspapers and most other news institutions, despite various feedback mechanisms, continue to be structured and to operate as transmission vehicles within large, impersonal corporate systems. Average citizens find it difficult, at best, to talk with news executives or even reporters and editors. Newsrooms operate behind doors often guarded by armed security agents, who insist on passes and identification. When people do get through, they find some journalists abrasive or arrogant—the ultimate "insiders," who are far more likely to interact with celebrities, bureaucrats, officials, authorities, and others who hold power than with a largely anonymous mass audience. Sharing the ownership of a story—that is, allowing a "source" or other interested parties to review an article before it is published—unsettles many journalists. They believe that if people have something to say about a piece, they should react in the same post hoc way audiences always have reacted, by writing letters to the editor or calling on the telephone.

While occasional stories result in tremendous response, most are met by silence, which explains why some journalists refer to their published articles as written in sand. They often receive little response from anyone outside their own families, friends, and news organizations. Journalists, of course, hope for a response—human interaction—whether or not they admit it. However, many mainstream news organizations make it difficult for people to respond. Editors frequently stay cloistered in newsrooms and reporters go where they can get information as efficiently and economically as possible—usually, as the beat system dictates, to official sources working in bureaucracies. Ironically many editors and reporters have little interaction with the people for whom they write and whose lives are altered by their news decisions.

Journalists can no longer afford to act as if they are conduits of information to an uninformed, and perhaps even unformed, public. They must develop new ways to listen as well as speak, to empathize, identify, and cooperate with citizens who, once included, will become more likely to say something of substance. In rhetoric, the oratorical mode was timely and appropriate in its age, but the new media have reasserted the primacy of the *interpersonal*. Politicians, evangelists, or journalists who lecture to us are gradually being replaced by those who are willing also to listen and speak with us. Print journalism has emphasized for decades a near-oratorical approach conditioned by the linear model—from privileged source to compliant receiver. That model will fail our times and conditions.

Developing a conversational journalism requires investing in educated reporters and editors, giving them time and opportunities to bring citizens into the conversation, and sponsoring innovative programs that help build a community which can act reasonably on issues and ideas. Some news organizations have moved in these directions. We think that, rather than cost more money, such changes will make more money. Newspapers are vital in active, vibrant communities where forums and catalysts exist for people's talk and opinions.

COMMUNITY

The word *community* enjoyed great popularity in the 1980s and into the 1990s, as critics, commentators, and ordinary people reminisced about the past or sought ways to bring people together in a more cooperative, harmonious existence (Nisbet, 1990). Community life usually appears friendlier and safer in our memories. Nowadays we frequently find our wished-for communities in crisis over racial divisions, crime, poverty, and other assorted ills.

Community can be defined superficially by geography, but in a deeper sense, community, whether a city, region, state, nation or other designation of place, comprises collections of interlocking subcommunities—families, churches, special interests, and associations of various sorts and sizes. A community of communities (Etzioni, 1993) allows for diversity and individuality, but ultimately all people within a larger community recognize that they share certain common conditions and fates. Even in communities torn by conflict, bonds remain as long as people communicate, whether in polite talk or heated argument. A community exists not through agreement, but through communication. Community disintegrates when communication access is strained, broken, or nonexistent.

By tradition and resources, news organizations are positioned to play a central role in maintaining, if not rejuvenating, community life. They provide communities with a common core of news, however imperfect, which is available to virtually all literate citizens, meaning that stories about Jesse Jackson are at least accessible to followers of David Duke, and vice versa. Moreover, if they so choose, news organizations further provide opportunities and means for people to learn and understand one another through public dialogue. For its part, journalism can, and often does, reinforce, enhance, and connect communication that occurs through a community's interpersonal and organizational channels. By marking and legitimizing the *conversational commons*, journalism contributes to communication links among people, groups, and places that were previously disconnected.

Market-oriented journalists, particularly at newspapers, recognize the multiple meanings of community and, as a result, tend to segment communities of place and association as categories of consumers, not citizens. So they produce zoned editions for neighborhoods or regions and special sections for seniors, teens, parents, women, churchgoers, business executives, and other "market groups." However, despite solid economic arguments in favor of "niche" journalism, that approach emphasizes differences rather than the commonalities of public life, such as communitywide values, priorities, and goals. Journalism should encourage and assist conversation within subcommunities, but its prime mission is to connect them within a larger community.

A journalistic commons based on a community in conversation with itself presents challenges. Big media in urban areas, where most of us live, cannot approximate the down-home flavor and familiarity of the weekly newspaper. Even in midsized cities, the chain-owned news outlets, which are managed by an upwardly mobile succession of news executives, often lack a community-based personality. However, an increased effort to connect through expressions of human concern will change the relationship of the news organization and its community, perhaps only subtly at first. News is shared, not dispensed. People recognize their stake in news; they want journalists to see, hear, and react to them. When news spotlights primarily the rich, powerful, vocal, and socially prominent and ignores, wrongs, or frustrates ordinary people, journalism and society pull apart. Journalism must remain aggressive in spotlighting social ills and holding public officials accountable, but in doing so, it must also give the larger community a voice.

Conversation binds communities, and conversation becomes our means—our eyes, voices, and ears—of discovering where we are going and where we have been. As journalists become full-fledged participants in the public dialogue, news will become a legitimated and sanctioned topic of conversation among all cultural groups, not just within an informed elite, and journalists will rightly be recognized as facilitators—not providers—of discourse. Conversation cannot be one-sided; at times, journalism must yield the floor, listening more and speaking less.

Within the environment of a conversational journalism, we are more likely to build an integrated, resilient, and tolerant society. Without a journalism that both speaks and listens within the civic dialogue, we will abandon democracy to the buffeting of social accidents. In the chapters that follow, we develop and exemplify these ideas, offering both an informal philosophy and a practical application of journalism based on the metaphor of conversation.

2 _____

The Conversation of Journalism:
A Metaphor for News

Strange as it seems in this day of mass communications, democracy still
begins in human conversation.
>   —William Greider (journalist), on "Frontline: The Betrayal of
>   Democracy," PBS, April 15, 1992

Journalism is a powerful social force, in part because it presumes
to take the people's perspective—and this presumption can
scarcely be overrated in explaining both its successes and its
failures. Journalism makes a difference at the level of everyday
existence, where people pay their bills, buy their lawnmowers,
argue with their children, and gripe about crooked politicians and
overpaid celebrities. At its best, journalism helps people to cope.
It is practical; it translates into results you can see and feel. At
worst, journalism is vulnerable to criticism aimed at this same
populist character, since it can trivialize and oversimplify an
increasingly complex culture.

The premise motivating this book is that journalism's practical
strength, which is rooted in its everyday utility, can provide a better
forum for intellectual excitement, civic conversation, and public

debate. Such a philosophy displays its own kind of practicality. We do not lay out a "how to" approach, designed to help journalists become better beat reporters, for example. Instead, we argue that journalism itself, in addition to its necessary discipline of internal self-engagement and self-assessment, should become a more responsive social force—in effect, it needs to enact a philosophy of the public sphere. Insight and outreach are mutually reinforcing, and journalism needs more of both.

CONDUIT JOURNALISM

Journalism in the information society can no longer characterize itself as a conduit. Merely informing cannot be its primary communicative goal. The mainstream news media work best as forces of social and cultural communication, with "conversation" as their defining metaphor. While investigating, uncovering, and informing are appropriate functions for any communicator, they must be balanced with corresponding functions of listening, negotiating, adjusting, and discovering through dialogue. A journalism dedicated to conversation defines news *relationally*, as a social process of negotiated meanings, rather than *objectively*, as a transmitted product. A "story" traditionally is a packaged, delivered artifact— an object or objective. Viewed within a broader context, a story is a complex implied relationship between communicators that, to some extent, is coauthored by all participants, senders and receivers alike—and with all the skills of communication, involving message creation and interpretation alike.

Unfortunately, while journalism concentrates on its packaging and aiming of the news, it struggles to enter the social dialogue that shapes the public's definition of what is interesting, relevant, and important. Its difficulty in connecting with people—in talking and listening to them—is ironic, perhaps even paradoxical, because journalism relies on the popular imagination and is interwoven into the common culture. Journalism's trivialized role in the public drama feeds those who attack the so-called media elite.

When Spiro Agnew and Dan Quayle as vice presidents labeled the media as an isolated cultural elite, they spoke from the vantage point of mansions, private school educations, the perquisites of high elected office, and personal wealth—all characteristics that are usually identified more with elitism than with the mundane circumstances of most reporters, columnists, editors, or producers. Yet for many citizens, the charges rang true. When journalism defines itself, at least by behavior, as a detached vendor of news and truth, it invites damning political attacks. In Western culture, the role of dispensing information is associated with power and authority. Conversely, the roles of listening and sensitivity are usually markers of reduced-status persons and groups, as feminists pointedly note.

Listening, when done well, is a potent relational force that cements relationships and proves that people have made a difference in the lives of others. Listening becomes more than the mere reception of communication messages; it becomes a message in itself, confirming the identities and importance of the speakers. Speech divorced from listening, no matter how graceful, is more empty than eloquent. In arguing against conduit journalism, we suggest that the profession should integrate more overtly both its speaking (information dissemination) and listening (interpretive) roles in the public conversation.

Other voices already have called on journalism to reconsider its role, so we are hardly alone. However, the change we encourage is both radical and fundamental. *Journalism actually must become a communication discipline*—which, ironically, is what it had thought it was all along. This redefinition is important for several interlocking reasons, which we develop in detail in subsequent chapters.

- The range of invitation of a redefined, conversational journalism will produce deeper and more comprehensive accounts of social issues, not just accounts of the events that are symptomatic of them.

- The inclusion and empathy characterizing a conversational journalism will be more suited to the needs and tensions of an era of multicultural diversity.

- The alignment of a conversational journalism with emerging communication and literary theories will encourage journalism's full partnership in the academic and scholarly dialogue.

- The ecumenical tone of a conversational journalism will ground it as a communication, and not just an information, discipline—fulfilling more nearly the vision for journalism and public life articulated by Dewey (1927) and others (e.g., Carey, 1989; Rosen & Taylor, 1992).

We subscribe to a definition of communication that moves beyond the concept of a linear transmission of intended meanings, with maximum fidelity, from point A to point B. Journalism literature often implies that communication is no more complex than transmission. According to James Carey, in fact, media research remains focused on the "transportation" metaphor for communication (1989). What, if not fidelity in transferring information, should be the defining characteristic of journalistic communication? Critic and poet Kenneth Burke, one of the Renaissance figures in the literature of this century, provided excellent clues in his discussion of *identification* as the basis for a "new rhetoric" (1967). Burke thought the philosophical ground for the "old rhetoric" was deliberate persuasion—the intentional attempt to aim messages so as to change an audience's attitudes and actions. The traditional approach exaggerates the intent and authority of the speaker or writer who attempts to deliver influence. At Burke's urging, however, audience needs receive greater attention. Communication, especially in a modern, mediated world characterized by the nearly instantaneous dissemination of messages and cross-cultural access of groups to each other, can no longer be dependent on message delivery and persuasion in the sense of the old rhetoric. Whereas the old rhetoric might have asked, "What can we say to change those people?" now communicators are challenged to as, "What can we find out about them that might increase our *identification* with them and ultimately, perhaps, our common alignment?" The difference is between doing to and doing with. Although both kinds of rhetoric share a concern with messages, audience analysis, clarity, stylistic force, and the influence of context, the old rhetoric is ill-equipped for the social subtleties and ethical dilemmas of a technological society. Its essence is monologue, not dialogue.

NEWS AS CONVERSATION

Equating journalism with conversation may at first seem odd or misplaced. After all, conversation suggests interpersonal, face-to-face activity, conducted across fences, at kitchen tables, at parties. A dictionary of communication terminology defines conversation as "informal talk; a type of interpersonal or small group interaction" (DeVito, 1986, p. 80). How, then, can an institution like the press engage in conversation? Though a small-town weekly might approximate its chatty tone, surely the *New York Times* and *U.S. News & World Report* are too distant from the interpersonal lives of their readers to converse—or are they? Inasmuch as conversation implies a specific set of appropriate "rules" and expectations within coordinated talk, it can become a powerful metaphor for other kinds of communication as well.

First, let us look not to metaphor but briefly to the literal interpersonal event we call conversation. In addition to its informality, conversation exhibits, says Nofsinger (1991, pp. 3–5), three other general properties. First, conversation is "fully interactive" in that it presumes a mutual recognition of its participants and a recognition of how each utterance contributes to a sequence of messages that are shaped by both what has been and what may be said. Conversation further presumes that all participants can speak and be heard, and thus, while not necessarily egalitarian, it is inherently empowering. Under such a definition, mandated or rote exchanges, such as hollow formalities, forced oaths or promises, and rituals, do not qualify.

Second, conversation is "locally managed": the outcome emerges from a particular interchange. Preordained rules (e.g., time limits, scripts, hidden agendas, masks, false roles, stipulated taboos) tend not to characterize conversation, although some exceptions, such as Bill Moyers's PBS interviews, might come to mind. Participants are in charge, operating without script or outside direction but within the implicit rules of language and culture. Conversants, therefore, are responsible to each other for the conversation. In such encounters, participants typically describe the conversation as having "a life of its own"; in effect, the conversational "life" grows in collaboration. Deborah Tannen (1989) noted that conversation is properly considered a "joint production," a "collusion," or an "ensemble" experience coordinated between speakers and listeners (pp. 10–14). Talking with another person, as Frederick Erickson observed, "is like climbing a tree that climbs back" (quoted in Tannen, 1989, p. 13).

Third, and expecially interesting in its implications, Nofsinger has shown how conversations are "mundane." Under normal circumstances, conversation seems to be nothing special. Its very "everydayness" makes the complexity of its underlying structure easy to overlook or underestimate. Since conversation is almost everywhere, it takes a special effort to unearth and disclose its pervasive effects on human expectation and behavior. For centuries rhetoricians studied "the trees" of human discourse when analyzing speech making and oratory, while social scientists have come relatively late to a study of "the forest" they were missing—everyday conversation. Nonetheless, conversation is the basis for more complex social organization. Jeremy Campbell (1982) concluded that "the proper metaphor for the life process may not be a pair of rolling dice or a spinning roulette wheel, but the sentences of a language, conveying information that is partly predictable and partly unpredictable. These sentences are generated by rules which make much out of little, producing a boundless wealth of meaning from a finite store of words; they enable language to be familiar

yet surprising, constrained yet unpredictable within its constraints"
(p. 12).

Conversation and journalism are, in a sense, companion concepts. Both depend on a connection to natural, everyday concerns
of communication; both depend on the ultrathin line between the
new and the familiar, between new news and old hat. Conversation
is important to journalism on several levels. One is journalism's
role in promoting conversation among people about their own
common involvement in public affairs—what we consider the
public conversation. In fulfilling a public conversational role,
journalists seek opportunities to stimulate or provoke people into
thinking, talking, and acting among themselves and to provide a
forum within which diverse voices and claims may be heard and
compared.

To support this engagement, journalists themselves must be
competent, active, and ethical on a second level: that of the
interpersonal conversation. Too often accused of aloofness and
arrogance, journalists must appreciate how much of the news
emerges from their own conversation with officials, authorities,
eyewitnesses, and "ordinary" citizens, rather than from interrogation or mere questioning. If the interview drives or stalls most news
stories, then the lack of training in interpersonal communication
within journalism schools is perplexing indeed (see Killenberg &
Anderson, 1976; Anderson & Killenberg, 1985).

A third level of conversation that is necessary to an involved
journalism is the *institutional conversation.* People who read or
hear the news must sense that the news organization is responsive—that it listens and is flexible and open to change as a result
of communicating with its public. This responsiveness does not
mean that news organizations should change shapes like amoeba
encountering new environments; nor does it mean that journalism
should neutrally adapt to mirror its public. Just as philosopher
Martin Buber (1965) showed that genuine dialogue cannot develop
when people lack identifiable positions or fail to stand their
ground, even while they consider seriously the other person's
ground, so, too, is dialogue impossible with chameleon institu-

tions. Through a genuine dialogue with a journalism grounded in strong and identifiable positions—which must also be adjustable and collaborative—citizens and journalists understand that journalism is not "theirs" and "out there," but rather, in many striking ways, is "ours."

THE TRADITION OF DESCRIBING SOCIETY AS CONVERSATION

A conversational metaphor for journalism is not a new and trendy intellectual trinket for the 1990s. Social commentators and scholars have a rich tradition of noticing the very bases of societies in the everyday talk of their members. In suggesting that journalism should pay closer attention to this tradition and to its own role within such historical continuity, we borrow from, and acknowledge, a variety of scholars who have understood social structures as forms of creative conversation.

Long ago, in *The Public and Its Problems*, John Dewey (1927) collected lectures in which he critiqued the modern condition and its potential threats to enlightened decision making. Dewey's warnings and insights are fresh today. He feared that social processes would become so technological and mechanized that human thought would emulate them. Thus, communication, which is the glue of a society, would simply become a means of telling people what to do and think. However, Dewey's concept of the public was far richer than this, and a "Great Society" was not automatically the "Great Community" toward which it could aspire. What might be lacking? Dewey offered this view:

> [In the "Great Community,"] . . . an organized, articulate Public comes into being. The highest and most difficult kind of inquiry and a subtle, delicate, vivid and responsive art of communication must take possession of the physical machinery of transmission and circulation and breathe life into it. When the machine age has thus perfected its machinery it will be a means of life and not its despotic

master. Democracy will come into its own, for democracy is a name for a life of free and enriching communion. It had its seer in Walt Whitman. It will have its consummation when free social inquiry is indissolubly wedded to the art of full and moving communication. (1927, p. 184)

Clearly, a merely intelligent and informed citizenry does not qualify as such a public or community. The citizenry must also become organized and, especially important in Dewey's scheme, "articulate." The "machinery of transmission"—even if it is accurate and thorough transmission of necessary information—is at best a first step toward the public that Dewey defined, and at worst, a pallid substitute for it. In addition to having something to speak about, a public must speak out and must speak back. In other words, a public must find itself enmeshed and implicated in conversation.

Dewey elevated conversation as the prototypical communication condition of a democratic public:

The winged words of conversation in immediate intercourse have a vital import lacking in the fixed and frozen words of written speech. Systematic and continuous inquiry into all the conditions which affect association and their dissemination in print is a precondition of the creation of a true public. But it and its results are but tools after all. Their final actuality is accomplished in face-to-face relationships by means of direct give and take. Logic in its fulfillment recurs to the primitive sense of the word: dialogue. Ideas which are not communicated, shared, and reborn in expression are but soliloquy, and soliloquy is but broken and imperfect thought. (1927, p. 218)

Dewey envisioned a society of conversationalists who encounter and respond to messages as participants, not as news consumers. News is not "made" and then "communicated" via journalism to an audience that then comes to "know" it. One of the intriguing implications of Dewey's conversational society is that journalism becomes less the conduit and more the context for the entire interactive process by which public audiences create news interactively. Dewey claimed that finding out something and knowing it are different things; knowledge depends on the ability to share and have access to what is "found out." It is not too hard to apply this point, by analogy, to the role of journalists in a mass society.

Dewey argued implicitly for a free press, but beyond freedom, he argued for a press that participates in a broad social conversation. Such journalism actively trusts and, in fact, helps create its own constituent audiences: "Dissemination is something other than scattering at large. Seeds are sown, not by virtue of being thrown out at random, but by being so distributed as to take root and have a chance of growth" (1927, pp. 176–177). As Duncan described (1962, p. 73), Dewey persistently tried to counter European philosophies that located unreason and irrationality in group responses—philosophies that distrusted the reactions of the so-called "common" people and instead trusted the actions of an authoritative, informed, and celebrated elite. Dewey, in contrast, asserted that "common" people, their senses of public communion, and the communication that knits together a society all have much in *common.* Genuine reason and informed rationality emerge from communication, not from authority—and if this claim sounds like a truism, it is because this pragmatic philosophy has taken hold in twentieth-century America, not because it has always been so elsewhere.

Dewey's philosophy represented a particular strain of American pragmatism that also motivated the social philosophers and sociologists who later came to be known as "symbolic interactionists" (see Duncan, 1962; Denzin, 1992). Much of the symbolic interactionist work past midcentury was grounded on the teachings of George Herbert Mead and his students, colleagues, and followers in the Chicago School (Mead, 1934, 1956). In fact, Dewey's influence on Mead was direct and pervasive.

Mead's contribution to modern communication theory was his unification of the sweeping range of human phenomena from inner speech through the organization of complex societies and cultures. Mead emphasized three concepts: mind, society, and self. Mind is the process by which individuals symbolically, through the medium of language, integrate and, in a sense, reproduce the complex structural dynamics of the larger society within their thought processes. A self is created when a person interacts with others in order to notice his or her differences from them. We do not tell ourselves who we are; rather, we interact with others as the only reliable means to discover who we seem to be to them. Through "the generalized other," Mead's hypothetical conception of the typical other person, people can anticipate how other persons may react to them. Clearly, Mead's ideas bridged psychology and sociology; thereafter, it would be difficult for scholars to consider them separately—or to want to do so.

To Mead, conversation is the essence of human endeavor. He used the term as a key image to explain the interrelated processes of mind, self, and society. People develop mature selves by learning to take roles, imagining what others might do within a game or future interchange, and rehearsing future action. This mature flexibility is dependent on the social order being a "conversation of gestures" (Mead, 1934, pp. 135–226; 1956, p. 212). To have a society is, therefore, to have a conversation.

Twentieth-century philosophers of dialogue have also made substantial contributions to the human sciences by implicitly presuming that conversation is the ideal or paradigm case of human communication. They do not define conversation literally as a face-to-face engagement conducted without plan or attention. Rather they stress the essence of conversation by which each participant speaks in order to invite a response that will be both heard and carefully considered. Any differences in their responses are presumed to be meaningful. Face-to-face conversation, then, becomes a broader model for explaining cultural development, socialization, and even *understanding* itself:

> The ability to understand is a fundamental endowment of man, one that sustains his communal life with others and,

above all, one that takes place by way of language and the partnership of conversation. (Gadamer, 1989, p. 21)

[We] ... come again and again to life, not indeed in those popular discussions which misuse the reality of speech, but in genuine conversation. If we ever reach the stage of making ourselves understood only by means of the dictograph, that is, without contact with one another, the chance of human growth will be indefinitely lost. ... Genuine conversation, and therefore every actual fulfillment of relation between men, means acceptance of otherness. (Buber, 1965, pp. 68–69)

As civilized human beings, we are the inheritors, neither of an enquiry about ourselves and the world, nor of an accumulating body of information, but of a conversation, begun in the primeval forests and made more articulate in the course of centuries. It is a conversation which goes on both in public and within each of ourselves. ... It is the ability to participate in this conversation, and not the ability to reason cogently, to make discoveries about the world, or to contrive a better world, which distinguishes the human being from the animal and the civilized man from the barbarian. ... Education, properly speaking, is an initiation into the skill and partnership of this conversation in which we learn to recognize the voices, to distinguish the proper occasions of utterance, and in which we acquire the intellectual and moral habits appropriate to conversation. And it is this conversation which, in the end, gives place and character to every human activity and utterance. (Oakeshott, 1959, p. 11)

Despite the different philosophical and political positions advocated by these scholars, they have much in common in emphasizing conversation as a central metaphor. Gadamer, Buber, Oakeshott, Burke (1957), Rorty (1979), Bakhtin (1981, 1986), and others, representing such diverse fields as anthropology (Crapanzano, 1992; Maranhao, 1990), social criticism (Ellul,

1985; Freire, 1970), education (Noddings, 1984), political science (Taylor, 1991), physics (Bohm, 1985), management (Senge, 1990), communication and linguistics (Carey, 1991; Stewart, 1978; Tannen, 1989), and sociology (Brown, 1987), have all advanced conversational dialogue as an important metaphor for the whole of social life, and not simply as a condition for cohesion. Some, like Gadamer, go beyond the metaphorical and simply pronounce conversation to be the ground of all language and, therefore, of all human experience.

CHARACTERIZING JOURNALISTIC DIALOGUE

Dialogue both exhibits and depends on certain characteristics (elaborated in Cissna & Anderson, in press). These characteristics suggest ways for journalism to begin to redefine its central mission to achieve a more democratically grounded conversational public.

Immediacy of Presence

Communicators are available to each other, and they strive to ensure that their messages are mutually accessible. They communicate willingly, not because they are bound by prior scripts or agendas. Colloquially speaking, communicators are "here" for each other (that is, in the same social space), and are "here" at the present time ("now") (Berger & Luckmann, 1966). French philosopher-psychoanalyst Jacques Lacan defined "empty speech" not as speech that seeks to say nothing, but as messages that do not invite or expect reply (Lacan, 1981).

A journalism that recites without inviting, that treats its content as a truth to be told and then digested, is founded on monologue. Though conversations will be held about it, as with any major news event, such as Hurricane Andrew in 1992, replies cannot be addressed in any meaningful way toward journalists. In fact, one could argue that linear, one-way, "transmission" news coverage cannot be defined as journalism in any meaningful sense.

Emergent Unanticipated Consequences

Although much of human communication necessarily is planned (imagine the chaos in a newspaper, for example, if the roles, rules, and procedures had to be reinvented each day), the contribution of dialogue always leaves room for surprise. It is this surprise—the intrusion of the unexpected—that illustrates why genuine learning is associated with the conversational realm. The surprise inherent in a democratic dialogue becomes the news on which a free press must thrive. To the extent that journalism becomes formulaic, its audiences understandably become passive, distant, and, ultimately, dismissive.

Recognition of "Strange Otherness"

No matter how much analysis of an audience takes place, and no matter how many reader and listener surveys are conducted, conversational partners cannot see, hear, or interpret the world in the same way. Although it is self-defeating to assume that an interviewer and interviewee inhabit thoroughly separated worlds, it is essential for them to recognize at some level that they cannot experience each other's perspectives fully. Presumably a language is shared, as are some cultural commonalities as well. However, many fundamental aspects of one person's experience will remain mysterious, unique, and "strange" in relation to the experience of another. For example, a young Latino woman assigned to interview Jesse Helms should anticipate the opportunities, and not just the difficulties, of the situation. In dialogic communication, the partners recognize the potential of an expanded repertoire of conversational content.

Collaborative Orientation

In dialogue, concern for self and concern for others are intertwined. To be involved in conversation means to recognize a common stake in outcomes, even when the individual goals seem separate or even antithetical. As Friedman (1974) pointed out, though, collaboration in dialogue does not preclude disagreement. Conflict is not necessarily the opposite of dialogue, and as quarreling couples often find when consulting a marriage counselor, heated exchanges in which each side is well heard by the other can be characteristic of a strong relationship. Similarly, managing editors know that if city editors are too acquiescent in a news meeting, important stories may be overlooked for the next day's paper. When dialogue includes disagreement, it approximates the dialectic of historical consciousness in which a higher (stronger, more solid, or emotionally and intellectually advanced) position can only be reached through the counterposing of thesis with antithesis; the resulting synthesis takes the communication system to a higher plane.

An important collaborative role of modern journalism lies in its ability to give voice to the voiceless. Due to social prejudice, many groups find themselves muted, with little access to avenues of decision making, and therefore unable to reach a stronger, more solid, or advanced position. In addition to developing its own voice, journalism can contribute to social dialogue by providing space for alternative voices to fuel the conversation while still maintaining their separateness and idiosyncratic identities.

Vulnerability

Conversational partners, as the previous characteristic implies, require a ground on which to stand—something to believe in—if communication is to improve. However, what happens when journalists dogmatically not only stand their ground but defend it with total certitude? "We stand by our story" can become a slogan or a tactic instead of a considered position. A conversation worthy of the name involves persons willing to let persuasive messages change their minds and adjust their actions. They can bear strong witness and assert themselves forcefully for what they believe is right, but ultimately, they develop the courage to say, "The other position may be right." The willingness to abandon a public position in favor of a better one amounts to strength rather than weakness.

Inflexibility, though, remains a potential problem with "watchdog" or "adversarial" journalism, in which journalists, by definition, are antagonists of the government and established power structures and adhere to the credo: "Comfort the afflicted and afflict the comfortable." Here, journalism assumes an automatic stance of opposition and suspicion with regard to government. Advocacy reporting leads to some important stories, but it also hampers journalism's ability to become a discerning yet receptive partner in the social conversation. Even when journalists are "right" in attacking government, if their avowed or perceived role is adversarial, their arguments can be dismissed too easily by opponents: "Of course the paper is critical; the media are out to get us."

Mutual Implication

Speakers and listeners, including writers and readers, create boundaries for each other. In a conversation, everything that is said can be assumed not only to characterize what a speaker thinks or intends; it may also reflect how the speaker judges or anticipates a listener. Listeners, for their part, develop an identity and learn who they are by interpreting how they are addressed. In turn, the extent of interpretation affects what they have at their disposal to say next.

Journalistic applications of this phenomenon arise in several contexts. Reporters sometimes fail to see their relationship to interviewees as "mutual implication" at all; they believe "the mayor won't talk about her campaign contributions" when, in fact, the mayor simply finds the reporter's attitude or listening skills poor and understandably chooses not to talk about the subject in that particular interview: "Here's a reporter who doesn't trust me; why should I trust her with my candid remarks?" Neither party might have intended such a result, and it may puzzle them both, but the outcome stands. A different interviewer and approach might have contributed to a fuller story, as experienced "good cop–bad cop" police interrogators and savvy reporters have discovered.

In a similar vein, cultural groups develop part of their sense of identity from how they are depicted in the media. Attributed identity can easily become self-fulfilling prophecy. The bases of a newfound multicultural awareness within journalism will continue to spring, we hope, from this insight. Journalists not only *report* but also *create* messages and thereby assume responsibility for them. They decide, for example, in which section to report an NAACP convention, how to describe racial characteristics of alleged criminals and victims, or whether to provide glowing coverage of the coming-out balls of white debutantes in a decaying city with a large minority population. This is journalism's shadow function: in a complex matrix of social life, journalism teaches people what to believe and how to feel about themselves and others. Society and journalism are mutually implicated, each contributing to the definition of the other.

Temporal Flow

True conversation cannot be analyzed apart from its past or its anticipated future. It is affected by the history of the communicators, both separately and together, and conversation speaks toward a future that must necessarily be considered malleable. Carey (1991) pointed out that conversation is a necessarily suspect activity within totalitarian societies. In Orwell's novel *1984*, for example, "there is cant and there is interrogation; there are furtive, stolen glances, and there are hurried coded messages. There is simply no conversation except in the pubs and the hidden room, and very little of it there. No danger Winston faces is quite as unnerving as that of starting a conversation . . ." (pp. 111–112). Conversation, Carey pointed out, connects people to memory, and it is memory that supports hope. True conversation requires trust in an open future and the belief that talk about ideas really can matter for the life of communities. Conversation enables a con-

tinuity of the past through the present and toward the future.
Human hope is maintained in this way, and, in a sense, only in this
way.

Genuineness/Authenticity

In a conversation that matters, each participant's contributions
are premised on an often unspoken assumption that what the
other person says corresponds to what he or she actually believes.
Of course, people do occasionally speak strategically from their
own self-interest or withhold some of what they know or feel.
However, to the extent that participants actively dissemble, a
conversation becomes progressively unlikely or even impossible. If unauthentic speech is taken as a norm, then conversation
in its truest sense is precluded, just as surely as American soldiers
were entertained by (while disbelieving and laughing at) Tokyo
Rose, and just as surely as used-car buyers often trade quips with
salespersons in the lot while each side knows that nothing of
significance will be said and nothing will be believed. The
exchange of untrustworthy messages, even under superficially
pleasant circumstances, does not qualify as conversation. At best,
it is a rather fruitless ritual. Some journalists will say, on occasion: "I don't care what people think of me. I'm just out here
to do my job." Such a view undermines a conversational model
of society, because whether one is trusted determines whether
another communicator or group will even bother to reply in cases
where they disagree or feel misunderstood.

The characteristics of dialogue outlined here depend on a commitment to communication maintenance. While much has been
made of the agenda-setting functions of media, we must be as
concerned with the maintenance functions. How can a society stay
on a relatively even keel while meeting its conflicts and tensions
directly? The concept of feedback in traditional information theory
allows analysts to measure the success or accuracy of previous
messages. If feedback functions to regulate a balance within a
system's operation, as cybernetic theory tells us, then any medium

of communication messages—or system of media—is a vital subset of system feedback for social maintenance. Journalism operates at the boundaries between our private and public lives, between citizens and the governmental, social, and corporate entities that claim to serve, but at times appear only to want to address or exploit, the public's consumer instincts.

Boundaries monitored by journalists should not be permeable in one direction only. If a society is to adjust to the competing demands of diversity, the larger social institutions must experience the impact of public reaction in ways that are comparable to those in which the public experiences the impact of corporate and political decision making. We propose that news organizations promote and sustain public communication by reaching out to a public that will otherwise lose its myriad (but uncoordinated) voices to organized lobbyists, special interests, celebrities, corporations, "spin doctors," and the menagerie of other authorities of conventional wisdom that crowd our pages and airwaves.

LIMITS OF A CONVERSATIONAL METAPHOR FOR JOURNALISM

Modern mass media and their supporting technologies have made meaningful human contact less likely, some critics claim. These commentators would find our theme of conversation a considerable conceptual stretch in analyzing the future of journalism. Ferrarotti (1988) argued that sophisticated media technology actually signals "the end of conversation," since the media now are encouraged to elevate themselves as power agents over their more proper mediating functions. To Ferrarotti, "The mass media do not mediate" but rather "restrict themselves to telling about themselves," thus becoming a "vocation for narcissism" (p. 13). Ferrarotti underscored an indictment that French social philosopher Ellul has made for years: technologically based media create an alien and antihuman "suppression of the subject," and "the distant relationship" comes at the expense of the intimacy of interpersonal life (Ellul, 1985, p. 49). Indeed, media systems can appear to stress one-way message transmission over two-way, or transactional, communication. Feedback is often deferred, diminished, or both. Citizens might be narcotized to think of themselves only as passive consumers of news, entertainment, advertising, and information.

Berger, Berger, and Kellner (1974) evoked a current social theme—homelessness—even though their critique of technology is now two decades old. Modern society is evolving into an ethic of interchangeability, in which social trends (including mass media) make people feel anonymous to the point that their jobs, their skills, and even their identities and relations are considered merely "packages," to be moved and manipulated to fit into social slots. Standard, official, expert sources in many news stories can usually be interchanged without affecting the content. They do not matter as people but only as objects. Berger, Berger, and Kellner's title, *The Homeless Mind,* provides a disturbing warning about our diminished potential for conversation; the human symbolic environment exists in a dialectical relationship with human identity.

Critiques of media technology that emphasize how mass media can diminish the human spirit seem to depend on the common assumption that unmediated face-to-face interaction is an "ideal type" of communication toward which other contexts should aspire (see Rafaeli, 1988, p. 128; Berger & Luckmann, 1966). Mediated communication, in this view, is inferior—a compromise at best, or a corruption at worst.

However, it is dangerous to romanticize the concept of conversation in analyzing media systems. Schudson (1978b) critiqued the assumption that mass media should accept an ideal of conversation as its criterion of effectiveness. Rather than believing that mass media unnecessarily compromise or corrupt interpersonal conversation, Schudson pointed to the communication compromises that are already inherent in everyday conversation. If conversation is an ideal, he suggests, then it is a flawed one. Conversation typically involves excessive triviality, misdirection, start-and-stop misunderstandings, shortcuts, strained silences, and even ritualized and stereotypical talk. As the ideal is usually stated, conversation, in fact, emerges as a Western, twentieth-century phenomenon. Earlier times and epochs did not seem to value conversational talk as we do today. Given these characteristics, it would seem that interpersonal conversation and mass-mediated communication simply involve different communication contexts, with neither necessarily serving as an ideal or desirable model for the other to emulate.

Schudson developed the notion that the conversational ideal itself could only have developed "in a world shaped by the mass media. Both the ideal of conversation, and its occasional realization, are in part a consequence of mass media" (1978b, pp. 325–326) because they have contributed to an "egalitarian" social climate and expanded the topics that are available for face-to-face discourse (pp. 326–327).

Schudson correctly concluded that the worlds of everyday talk and technological media are necessarily different and should not be judged by the same criteria. Criticizing media for not being face-to-face conversation is futile, and conversation itself is usually not a transcendent experience of wisdom, creativity, and insight. Surely, however, Schudson would not have us renounce ways to integrate into our media theory the potential advantages of what we could term conversation at its best. Early in his argument, Schudson isolated such attributes of the ideal as continuous feedback, spontaneity, and egalitarian assumptions, showing how each is violated in many conversations. This is fair enough, and certainly true enough, yet he still seems to assume that feedback, spontaneity, and equality can in fact improve either unsatisfactory conversation or media news. The new electronic media, compared with older forms, tend to *heighten* the sense or experience of shared human presence while communicating, moving toward the potential (and not the triviality and compromises) of conversation (Rafaeli, 1988; Rice & Associates, 1984; Anderson, in press). At the very least, Schudson provides a practical reminder that we should not romanticize the concept of conversation, for conversation has limits, too. However, it does not appear to diminish, in the final analysis, the value of the metaphor of conversation.

A related limitation to a conversational metaphor should be recognized. It is increasingly difficult to survey the social scene without regarding the relative and contingent markers of power that influence communication, often in exceedingly subtle ways. When a particular race, gender, or ethnic group's reality dominates society essentially without challenge as the sanctioned view, then a warpage of conversation occurs through "meaning monopoly" (Rommetveit, 1987, p. 98). We see this condition when a noted scholar delivers an incomprehensible lecture and no one asks questions despite persistent invitations to respond, or when a network anchor asks uninformed questions in a panel interview show but no one alludes to the mistakes. We also observe a meaning monopoly when men interrupt women in the conference room or dismiss their ideas without really hearing them, and we see it in a news-delivery system that claims to be reporting what happens day-to-day but does not provide for adequate participation from readers and viewers. Sparse public reactions, which may be published as letters to the editor or flashed on the screen at the end of a "60 Minutes" broadcast, usually are boiled down to little more than messages stating, "You are right" or "You are wrong." While this process of registering replies may seem interactional, if not conversational, the power relation is evident: the boundaries or rules are set by the organization, which invites and uses the response at its discretion.

Invitations to conversations on any interpersonal, institutional, or cultural level necessarily have power implications, which have been explored recently by critical theorists (Hall, 1989; Grossberg, Nelson, & Treichler, 1992). In many contexts, conversation allows people to cooperate and even reach consensus, but in others, the power relationship (e.g., boss over employee, teacher over student) stifles candid communication. Conversational dialogue develops when people expect and accept the *otherness* of each other, give it credence, and then speak from their own ground. Without such acceptance, or with it muddied, meaningful response deteriorates. Remember that sociologists typically have defined social power as the ability to effect outcomes even against the resistance of others. When respondents are confronted with such power, they often censor themselves. Although vigilant journalists can be a powerful positive force for dialogue, they are often restrained by their own sense of role ambiguity: "For whom do I speak? Or do I merely report?"

Dialogue can also mollify and pacify the powerless, and this also may be seen by some as a limitation of a conversational model. Psychologist Richard Farson observed that it is no accident that labor unions historically have been suspicious of attempts by consultants to involve them in informal encounter-type groups with management (Farson, 1978). They believe that the power-based reality of their situation is such that when encountering the arrayed economic power of the company, the union needs a certain psychic distance, which dialogue could erode. "Please do not make us see and empathize with the other side's *human* side," they seem to plead. "We have too little going for us already. Do not further erode the basis that sustains our own group's solidarity." It is not difficult to see the same reasoning at work in various groups' objections to some inner city community-building programs or in the American Indian, African-American, or Asian-American communities. After the nationwide unrest following the 1992 riots in South Central Los Angeles, a number of African-American leaders wryly observed that integration had indeed worked at some level; it had worked "so well," in fact, that such significant black urban presences as the church and school had been thinned out, often moving to the suburbs, making it difficult to mobilize and lead an ideological struggle based on real racism. Thus, in one sense, increased dialogue and interaction can undercut a particular group's influence and its ability to demand justice.

Scholars and students of communication need not necessarily subscribe to such an analysis to recognize its potency. Moreover, journalists who engage in the delicate balancing act that is news do not require lectures about power relations. They themselves are too often the objects of scorn, envy, or attributed power. Like it or not, even while attempting to be neutral facilitators of dialogue, journalists will forever be branded as subversives or as govern-mental apologists.

The conversation of journalism is necessarily a conversation about journalism in which no answers are automatic or easy. Certainly, the remainder of this book will not package and peddle answers. In the spirit of questioning that Gadamer (1982) says underlies all dialogue, however, we hope to inquire, probe, and offer alternate perspectives on how journalism can contribute to a society that ultimately will attempt to talk with itself, whether or not journalists participate.

3

News and Realities:
Exploring Practice and Promise

News is what people talk about, and news makes people talk. Yet newspapers publish millions of words that stimulate little talk and no interest, and to the extent that people quit reading or attending to the news, that is a profound dilemma. News, as we have come to know it, fails to engage many people, which they acknowledge by not buying papers, not watching traditional network news shows, flocking to radio talk shows, buying alternative publications, and watching pseudo–news shows and "reality" programs on TV.

Newspapers in the last decade fluffed up graphics, redesigned pages and sections, and started programs designed to get the public involved. Some reorganized newsrooms to get more and different perspectives and ideas and redistribute work loads and responsibilities. Several have cut back international, national, and state reporting to concentrate their resources on local and community news. Projects abound that attempt to put the paper in touch with its own readers and community, and thus to engage the public in a conversation.

Eventually, these efforts may succeed and spread. In the meantime, most current news looks a great deal like news has looked since the Penny Press. Those who create and produce it seem bound by persistent conventions, traditions, definitions, and routines and fated to repeat their histories and perpetuate their mistakes. It is not for lack of criticism. Will Irwin, Walter Lippmann, Louis Brandeis, Upton Sinclair, the Kerner and Hutchins commissions, H. L. Mencken, A. J. Liebling, I. F. Stone, and others have pointed out numerous contradictions, absurdities, inequities, biases, and assorted conscious and unconscious problems in news.

Privacy, press arrogance, education of reporters, truth, fact, objectivity, ethics, and many other major issues have been debated for decades. Insightful documents, such as the report on mass communication by the Commission on Freedom of the Press (Leigh, 1974), have explored the strengths and weaknesses, offering guidelines and directions for a more diverse, responsive, and responsible mass communication environment. It is unfair to say the press ignores all criticism because, like news, criticism's complexity makes it difficult to determine what is worth considering.

This chapter explores some of the conventional, objective, commercial, and ideological characteristics of news and suggests some of their influences. Despite efforts to change, news remains largely confined to conventional boundaries. News emphasizes government and authority, leaders and celebrities, thereby limiting its range and access. It has a comfortable familiarity reinforced through consistent structure, presentation, and stereotype.

The most pervasive claim made about U.S. news is its supposed objectivity. Beyond certain verifiable facts, however, news is not and cannot be objective in the sense that it is without human bias, although it can and must be fair. Forcing news into this objective mold drastically limits its content and expression, discouraging and devaluing participation by the public journalism purports to serve.

News in a capitalist society cannot escape influences from the bottom line. Economic considerations shape the form, content, and presentation of news, though the extent of such influences is usually excluded from the news itself. Recognizing the vast economic influences and making them part of the conversation can help journalists and the public understand and perhaps modify the role of economic decision making in news.

Critics have analyzed news from various political and ideological perspectives with mixed results. Most, in one form or another, argue that news reflects and therefore reinforces the dominant ideology, in part by underestimating its audience. Vast changes in information technology, altered attitudes about democratic participation, and an uncertain economy may have opened the way for a different kind of journalism, one that encourages and legitimizes participation by citizens rather than informs and entertains consumers.

BOUNDARIES: OLD AND NEW

To say news is complex understates the problem. Every semester, journalism students struggle through assignments to "define news," handing them in to professors who are themselves unsure how to define news. Those students generally rely on the same conventional wisdom, reiterating qualities or attributes in virtually every news-reporting textbook and reporter's head—timeliness, proximity, consequence, conflict, prominence, and human interest. Some academic treatises on news offer more sophisticated terms and explanations, but the result, in most cases, is consistently conventional news.

Definitions of news inexorably lead to the way in which the press reports news and the content of the news it reports. Textbook definitions encourage us to think about surface phenomena: something dramatic, emotional, that happened recently, close by, involving or affecting people of importance or large sums of money or many people. Reporters, in fact, cover the news, as, for example, paint covers the basement wall: a thin, functional, perhaps decorative, surface layer hides whatever is underneath. In a way, the attributes internalized by reporters provide only minimal criteria for news. The attributes, at least as they are taught in classrooms, simplify news decisions, usually resulting in simplistic news. Once an event or issue passes the threshold that makes it news, reporters need not explore further (although, of course, some do).

Critics often attack news for what it is not, which leaves vast areas vulnerable to attack. If a dog biting a man is not news but a man biting a dog is, then news is what is odd or different; what is normal or the same is not newsworthy. That means that most of life is not news and, therefore, rarely becomes part of the public conversation. If Walter Lippmann (1922) correctly described news as the spotlight, then most of life remains in the dark. If news is just what breaks the surface, then what remains below will go untold or undetected. If news is timely, then much of what happened the day before yesterday is not news. If news is important or significant, then the unimportant or insignificant do not qualify. That means, in turn, that most of what people do is considered unimportant and insignificant. If news focuses on conflict and change, then peace and stability are not news. If news is basically "what went wrong," then most of what is right will not make the news. If most news is made by people who are important, then the rest of us are unimportant because, by definition, we rarely make news. Are we willing to live with the social consequences of these messages?

Hartley (1982) defined news in terms of *frequency*, the timespan of both events and their meanings; *threshold*, the size of an event; *unambiguity*, clarity of an event; *meaningfulness*, cultural proximity or relevance; *consonance*, predictability of or desire for an event; and *unexpectedness*, an event's unpredictability or rarity. These somewhat different perspectives still describe conventional news—quick, big enough to be noticed, simple, culturally and socially relevant, and expected. A shoot-out in the street is more likely to be included in the news than a series of articles exploring conditions that might lead to community violence.

Even relatively complete lists never satisfactorily define what news is, though they are used to define its boundaries. Journalists use these and other conventions to judge newsworthiness. The attributes alone or in combination mean little. Timeliness, proximity, conflict, drama, or emotion, for example, could easily apply to working-class families faced with economic, school, religious, and other crucial decisions, but the experience of ordinary people is rarely news, even though the decisions they must make are of great import. Their decisions become news if something happens to bring an issue or problem to the fore, such as a new government policy or a large protest. A family or families might be used to illustrate the dimensions of a problem in a news article, but rarely more than once, and then usually at the height of reporting of the issue. As other issues emerge to occupy the news, families still decide to declare bankruptcy, sacrifice a child's education for food on the table, or suffer through abuse or neglect, and they do so silently, often anonymously, and certainly without making news. They are the same decisions that once made news, consuming as many or more people, changing lives, rending families, draining finances, yet we do not call these private experiences news.

News necessarily excludes most people, just as it excludes most situations. It has focused primarily on *the important*, and it has defined "official," "authoritative," "widely known," and "expert" as such. In a sense, news has become society's stage, its everyday Broadway or Hollywood. It is filled with officials, socialites, celebrities, experts, authorities, leaders, people who speak for groups and organizations, deviates, lawbreakers, con artists, the rich and powerful. They fill the news because the usual attributes assigned to news and the way in which journalists use them require that the "usual suspects" be sources and subjects. A teacher's colon operation is not news, but a political leader's surgery is—only the latter is important by news definitions. Lunch at a local restaurant by an out-of-town welder is not news, but lunch at the same restaurant by a visiting movie star or other celebrity often is. The welder is an ordinary citizen whose visit is routine; the celebrity is, as Daniel Boorstin (1961) once wrote, a person who is well known for well-knownness, an "important" person whose visit is not routine but rather unexpected and novel.

The point is not that all colon operations and restaurant lunches should be news, but that we need to reexamine the shape of our definitions. Why is the political leader's colon surgery news and the teacher's not? The politician is theoretically in a position of power and influence, and his or her life-threatening surgery could affect many people. Why is the celebrity's visit to the restaurant news and the welder's not? People have been taught to be curious about the celebrity because he or she is famous. Why is the celebrity famous? The fame comes from media attention. Curiously, our current situation is one in which the news must cover what has been legitimized as news by repeated past practice.

Most news outlets continually provide news similar to the leader's surgery and the celebrity's visit. News attributes and conventions almost require that these be reported, and conveniently, they are relatively simple and inexpensive, requiring little time or expertise. In each case, press agents might furnish almost all the information needed. But what of the teacher and the welder?

News recognizes the power and influence of politicians but not necessarily of teachers. Politicians are elected, make news, and presumed to have power; they serve a defined public in defined ways. The teacher is not widely known or in the same public ways accountable to the public; a teacher's successes and failures are difficult to measure and rarely publicized. However, when incremental and cumulative effects are considered, the teacher may be more influential than the politician, and all teachers combined may be more influential than all politicians combined. Nonetheless, the politician's operation is automatically presumed to be newsworthy and the teacher's is not.

The contributions of welders and celebrities are not parallel in the way that those of teachers and politicians are, though if we had to choose a world in which one role or the other immediately vanished, the decision would not be automatic. Furthermore, if the restaurant and the town depend on an influx of visitors, it is less easy to gauge the importance of the visits. While publicizing the celebrity's visit might encourage more people to visit, the welder represents all the people who do, or could, regularly visit.

By deciding what and who is news, the press emphasizes some values over others. We do not argue that news determines values, because media content must be analyzed in the context of society, culture, and environment, yet news remains the most consistent source of information that people consider reliable, truthful, and accurate. Therefore, its values certainly affect and reflect our values as citizens. In the world of news, people with power, authority, and celebrity prevail over the weak, disenfranchised, and unknown. The rich prevail over the poor, the official over the unofficial, the knowledgeable over the ignorant, the smart over the stupid, the attractive over the plain, and the vocal over the voiceless. The important prevails over the common, the unexpected over the routine, the dramatic over the casual, and so forth, through the list of attributes. The news also bestows authority and defines and bestows importance in some cases, while at the same time, it withholds authority and importance in others.

Not everything can be news, so something has to be omitted. Perhaps the teacher's colon operation or the welder's trip to the restaurant should not be reported individually in the news, but that does not mean that the teacher, the welder, and so much of the rest of the public need be invisible, represented only as statistics, referred to as part of the "mass" audience (or as consumers, readers, or viewers). News outlets attempt to include "ordinary" people, but these often, unintentionally yet uncomfortably, mimic television's "Real People" or home video programs in which ordinary people do weird things for a few seconds of fame. Most news outlets have not realized their potential to engage individual members of the public, nor have they recognized people's potential for valuable, vital, and necessary contributions to the conversation of news.

We do not contend that all mundane events be defined as "news," but only that the activities and talk of everyday people should be given greater recognition as important. News can, and perhaps should, be about what people do: the human condition or human affairs. Given a voice, people become part of the conversation. Many are excluded now, in part because definitions of news and people's perceptions of it remain encapsulated in traditional molds. Public affairs reporting involves affairs of the public, but usually from a perspective of government, business, or the institution. Just as the study of complex organizations has evolved from an almost exclusive focus on management decision making to a newer, more inclusive focus on the everyday talk that sustains what is termed "organizational culture," so, too, must news temper its infatuation with politicians and celebrities. "Public affairs" as "human affairs"—news of the human condition—directs emphasis unmistakably to the things people do to give meaning to their lives—to their obstacles and triumphs—and broadens the scope of what can be reported as news.

A conversation of journalism opens up possibilities far beyond official actions of government bodies, political leaders, and the actions of large organizations and institutions. Such news reporting adjusts our notions of importance, proximity, timeliness, and other traditional attributes. Events might be important not in and of themselves, but because they illustrate what people endure or celebrate daily, and people might be important not because they are officials, leaders, or authorities, but because they are interlocking parts of an event. If the news made a place for people's enduring struggles, their little triumphs, and the daily interactions that give their lives meaning—their humanity—then proximity might become more than just physical or geographic closeness, as people are tied together by more than space. Moreover, the moments illustrating or even defining our humanity—absorbing insults, facing up to authorities, signing up for or leaving welfare, getting mugged, passing the high school equivalency exam, getting a loan, moving, falling in or out of love—are important not because they just happened, but because they speak to our values and our lives, no matter when they occurred. In contrast to the usual news criteria, this approach emphasizes nontraditional attributes such as perspective, context, completeness, and enduring human values.

Newspapers in the late 1700s and early 1800s published stories that taught lessons about greed, love, faith, constancy, and other qualities of being human. The stories often had little or no anchoring in time, and if true, could have happened the previous week, year, or century. They were not important because they were recent, timely, or even true (although most readers no doubt thought them so); they were important for their content, and the lessons or morals derived from it. That is, they were published to contribute to a better, more interactive public—not because of a simple impulse to *report* what happened. Because they were published in newspapers, we study them as news, and as news, they represent a far different definition of what is important than news today.

Offering insights into the human condition has to be more than a feature or story here and there. We cannot say: "OK, here's the story on the human condition. Now we don't have to do that again for awhile." Reporting human affairs brings in a multitude of voices, including the paper's own, as part of a conversation about people and how they survive or thrive in the community. Providing insights into the human condition is different from providing the truth about the government, providing a complete record of the city council meeting, or doing many other things that fall under traditional definitions of journalism. We need not abandon conventional news, but we can supplement it and remove it from its pedestal.

Suggestions that reporters rely less on official sources and more on ordinary people, less on policymakers and more on people affected by the policies, often go nowhere because it is impossible to find people who accurately can speak for all women, all blacks, all white males (though it is all too easy to find those who *will* do so). The press would not need so many official statements or spokespeople if indeed news were seen as helping provide context for the human condition. The press needs official statements from official people when it hands down official versions. Even then, it is ludicrous to allow one spokesperson, or even several, to sum up the opinions of all black or white people, all brown, yellow, or red people, all women, all gun owners, or any group. Nonetheless, news organizations validate, cultivate, and depend on a handful of such representatives because the definitions and conventions of news require it.

Moving away from the tyranny of official sources requires bringing more diversity into the news arena. It means supplementing the official perspective (sometimes seen as the true or even only perspective) with several others. A conversational journalism is a pluralistic journalism.

Journalism should provide people with opportunities to see familiar things, governmental actions and pronouncements, for example, in fresh and unfamiliar ways. Making the familiar strange is generally a province of art. News tends to make almost everything familiar by enveloping the novel with familiar forms and contexts. It might be argued that this is one of the appeals of news as it appears in newspapers and television. Despite mayhem, violence, revolution, and chaos in the world, news is constant, consistent, and orderly—everything has its place and little happens to change that. The paper is in the yard or mailbox at the same time each morning. It is comforting to know that the same kinds of articles will be in the same sections, or in the same order on television, day after day, week after week, and month after month, no matter what happens. The world is skewed and crazy, but the packaging and presentation of news is orderly and sane. Articles, too, fall into familiar, comforting, rhythms and patterns, with the most important information in the first paragraph and the least important in the last.

In its content as well, news offers pronounced villains and heroes, ostensibly as the source of most of our bad and good fortune. The news often breaks exceedingly complex issues, such as inflation, economic growth, civil rights, health care, into digestible pieces characterized by personal conflict and motivation. We do not have to understand inflation if we can know the personalities promoting opposing policies designed to affect inflation. Ross Perot voters in the 1992 presidential election, for instance, told interviewers they were not sure what Perot would *do* about the economy if elected—but that they were sure he was the kind of man to back his promises to "get under the hood." Further, certain words serve as codes to evoke certain images: "urban renewal," "transitional neighborhood," "Korean shopkeeper," "Jew," "football player," "supermom," "corporate executive." Stereotypes, while necessary, provide easy shortcuts, and whether conscious or unconscious, they contribute to the familiarity and comfort of the news environment. Writers can avoid elaborate explanations by plugging in a code word or stereotype to relay messages that many people might readily understand (though not all in the same way).

News is comfortable, for those who write it and for those who read or hear it. By making it less familiar, breaking old rules, and moving outside old formulas, we make it less comfortable, which might be dangerous, if exciting. News will not usually be art, but news that breaks away from conventions and traditions might creatively infuse new perspectives into old debates, stir thoughts, and invite wider participation in the public drama.

BEYOND THE OBJECTIFICATION OF NEWS

Objectivity is the enduring myth of journalism. Its shrouded origins have never clearly emerged from the hundreds of studies and discussions of wire services, the telegraph, the scientific method, capitalistic enterprise, the search for community, and many other factors that no doubt contributed to the evolution of objective news in the United States. Journalists struggle to provide objective news—news with as little bias and as much "truth" as possible. This brings up philosophical, and other, dilemmas. Can news or any other human communication be objective or without bias? What do we mean by truth?

Most journalists think that news is objective; they would argue that they try to be as unbiased as possible. Moreover, though they might not think about it in these terms, most see a world that has an objective reality—a world that has a concrete truth that can be reported faithfully and perhaps even reflected or mirrored. Consequently, when reporters cover school board meetings, for example, they return with articles that they think come close to reflecting "what happened" at those meetings. They believe the meetings were news events and that by covering them, they gathered the news and wrote articles that presented what happened truthfully, accurately, and fairly, thereby providing their readers with an objective record of the meetings.

From another perspective, we might assume that reporters cannot be objective because no objective reality exists ready to be gathered. Instead, reality is composed of *human perceptions* of what is happening. In what social scientists refer to as the social construction of reality, journalists create or produce news; the reporter's decisions determine what to report, who to interview, what to ask, what to record, what to include in the article, what to emphasize, and so forth. Journalists essentially construct the article, and therefore the news. They do not fabricate its raw materials, but they do shape and determine, every step of the way, what is told and what is not.

Whatever constitutes reality does not present itself in forms convenient for mass media news, for human events seldom happen in most-to-least important order and generally lack clear beginnings, middles, and ends. These are, essentially, artificially created from the existing chaos of facts, assertions, events, pseudo-events (made only to be reproduced), emotions, and so forth. Even a life cycle is not a complete "story," though the biography might start at birth and end at death, because important elements, including influences on the subject of the biography, occur before birth and after death. A lifetime is not a time line. A lifetime is unfathomably complex, webbed with myriad events, thoughts, obstacles, emotions, values, attitudes, and interlocking influences. A biographer builds an account out of choices made from available versions of different negotiated realities, which accounts for drastically conflicting interpretations of the same life by different biographers.

In many ways, the reporter faces a comparable task after attending the school board meeting, which is itself not a complete "story," even though the news article might "cover" its duration. But what happened before the meeting might affect, or even determine, some happenings at the meeting. In addition, what happens at public meetings affects people, sometimes drastically, well beyond the physical site of the meeting and well beyond any reporter's ability to anticipate the outcome. Some articles, despite inherent difficulties and complexities, attempt to reflect such circumstances, but too many define the news narrowly as *what happens during the meeting*. Reporters, relying on news values, tradition, convention, routines, practice, perception, socialization, training, and sometimes ideology, deem certain items important and others not, deciding which are worth reporting. Often, besides reporting actions taken, the article bears little resemblance to the actual meeting, which can include long, boring interludes, comments by audience members labeled as crackpots, asides from one board member to another, outbursts of laughter, and any number of other things that are never recorded. In that sense, the person's life and the school board meeting, no matter how neat and complete they seem, must be constructed by a variety of journalistic decisions before they appear as a biography or news article. That reporters sometimes efficiently, automatically, and unthinkingly accomplish this construction of news should be a cause for concern, not a badge of professionalism. (Some reporters even boast that most of their stories are more than half written by the time they arrive at the scene.)

Considering objectivity in journalism forces, in turn, consideration of the slippery nature of "facts" and "truth." Reporters go out to "get the story," which is not always the same as getting the news and certainly not the same as getting the truth or even the facts, although the public and the newsroom often think of them as the same. What is a news fact? How is one captured? Romano (1987, p. 62) quoted Ridder (1980): "A fact merely marks the point where we have agreed to let the investigation cease" (p. 62) and Richter (1978): "Facts are the shadows that statements cast on things" (p. 9).

News facts are indeed shadowy. Some might argue, for example, that an accurately produced quote is a fact. If the mayor said spending by the city was less this year than last year and the reporter quoted the mayor in an article to that effect, that quote constitutes a fact for many readers. If the mayor produced figures from last year showing how much the city spent, the reporter could cite that as a fact in an article. If the mayor produced a budget showing how much the city planned to spend this year, the reporter could cite that as a fact as well. These examples do not nearly exhaust the range of possibilities, but which of them are truly facts? The mayor's quote might be untrue, last year's budget may be inaccurate, and this year's budget may be speculative. In each case the journalists would have reported a "fact" which, after publication, turned into something quite different.

Journalists, as a rule, cannot be responsible for the accuracy of every statement they quote in articles and, especially in political reporting, they may include quotations they know to be false or at least highly exaggerated. When they quote statistics "proving" opposite points on the same issue from opposing candidates, they know that at least one set is wrong. Fact and truth create the same dilemma of definition. For example, it may be that it is a fact—it is true—that the Bulls beat the Rams 21–20 in the state championship. It may be true that two players on the Bulls scored the three touchdowns and one kicker scored all three extra points. For both teams, the usual statistics—the score, yardage gained and lost, interceptions, and fumbles—are usually verifiable by comparative observations, even though the people keeping statistics make mistakes, consciously and unconsciously. It might be argued that if sports reporters confined articles to those kinds of statistics, articles would be, by most definitions, factual and true.

However, articles about most games contain more than bare statistical coverage. We are told of momentum shifts and other team and individual psychological states, crucial plays and series of downs, coaches' and players' viewpoints and comments, reporters' and columnists' analyses of what went right and wrong, and speculations of all kinds. These, inasmuch as they purport to tell us what happened, are not verifiable, nor are they necessarily true. At best, they are informed guesses or interpretations based on special knowledge. They frame reality so that audience interpretations are more likely to be coherent and meaningful.

These same observations apply to elections as well as football games, in part because throughout much coverage these events resemble each other, but mostly the observations apply to virtually all news. For example, generations of students now have learned the dubious "fact" that John Kennedy defeated Richard Nixon for president in 1960 because of a televised debate in which Nixon looked weary, unshaven, and perhaps faintly unsavory. In this way, folklore and guesswork, repeated often enough with confidence, assume the status of fact.

A vast and varied public can agree on many things. The Bulls and the Rams played a game and the Bulls won. We can agree on most statistics. To that extent, reporters can be objective. A sports reporter, no matter how much he or she loved the Rams, would be exceedingly foolish to report in the paper the next day that the Rams won. He or she could, however, write a story in such a way that the Rams appeared to have been cheated by officials, hurt by key injuries, played better than the Bulls, or valiantly fought a far superior team. Such an article can be framed in numerous ways. The point is that beyond the facts that can be proved or shown to be true, news is largely speculative and interpretative—a constructed reality.

Most reporters attempt to harness the speculative nature of news by attempting to write fairly and honestly. In the football story, beyond the verifiable statistics, what constitutes objective reality? If the coach and several players on one team think a certain play was the turning point of the game, is it indeed the turning point? Would not the other team have to agree as well? How much of this consensus is necessary before such assertions can be made? What in the game, aside from statistics, can we say constitutes a reality on which all can agree?

There is little on which to agree, argue the social constructionists. We invent key elements of that game for ourselves, in our various groups. Moreover, while journalists might have some special training to see things in ways that the general public might not, they, too, because they are human, create the game for themselves. That is not to say that 100,000 fans and 500 reporters witnessing a game will report 100,500 different versions, but neither will they all agree on every point. In effect, to social constructionists, no single game existed, and if these theorists are correct, we might say that the dilemma of the journalist is that he or she will report on several of them and ignore several others in creating only one cohesive account.

That we report on some of many possible situations is true of most news, and it results in, among other things, some distrust of a press that many people feel is arrogant, untrustworthy, and inaccurate, or at least biased. In a sense, however, this is a dilemma only to the extent that journalists insist they are delivering the Truth, the official and perhaps only definitive version of an event. It is the kind of attitude illustrated by frequent and loose use of the phrase, "We stand by our story," as though it were the only possible one.

Providing "both sides" of an issue, or sometimes even several sides, does not by itself make a news article objective and unbiased, and it certainly does not provide people with a complete view of an issue. Often, when news organizations have covered the abortion issue, for example, they make sure that the anti-abortion versions of events and issues are offset by the pro-abortion versions. This bipolar decision to stack the deck into two piles is usually called balanced coverage. Even if coverage is weighted somehow in favor of one side, the news is dominated by those adamantly for or adamantly against, whereas most people fall somewhere in between.

Most people do not demonstrate on either side and many harbor conflicting feelings and emotions, often feeling opposed to both extremes. News defined as current, significant, important, and filled with conflict and human interest rarely explains the social ambivalence of such issues. Abortion usually gets covered when "antis" and "pros" meet in some dramatic conflict, the more physical the better, but day after day, women (and often their families) struggle to decide to have or reject abortions, follow through on those decisions, and face the consequences of their actions.

Reporting protests, arrests, violence, and conflicts at clinics that perform abortions probably will not help most people clarify the abortion issue in their own minds, yet most news organizations cover "abortion" almost exclusively under these circumstances, which conveniently lend themselves readily to "two-sided" coverage. Other less charged issues, including environmental concerns, business markets, and most Republican-Democrat political issues, receive this approach as well. Greenpeace and other environmental activism groups have learned that to the American media, confrontations are newsworthy in ways that reasoned advocacy is not. In most cases, the issues are not covered at all, only the more newsworthy or easily identified or measured circumstances, including protests, violence, personalities, and conflict. Two-sided coverage is the journalists' insurance policy against charges of bias—it is automatically balanced and demonstrably "objective." With it, journalists keep themselves blameless while providing opposing and dramatic viewpoints from easily accessible, usually authoritative sources.

Two sides cannot represent the range of possible positions on social issues, and by offering two opposing, and often canned, practiced, and entrenched, viewpoints, journalists clarify neither people's struggles over the issues nor the public dialogue. The two-sided approach kills more discussions than it fosters; even presenting multiple sides of an issue, as long as news is packaged as Truth in definitive articles, does little to encourage people to debate issues or offer more than their own surface evaluations and put-downs.

The two-sided model would pose fewer problems if journalists and their readers were regularly reminded the news is only one version (perhaps even an authoritative version) of an event. It might be an important or even influential version, but it is still one that does not close the subject and shut down debate. News articles are most appropriately considered as contingent messages contributed to the public conversation, ones that could be sharpened, or rounded, even substantially altered, and certainly explored by a variety of subsequent voices. This invitational or forum quality of news means that a "story" or issue is kept alive in the press by people's ideas and comments in the conversation, rather than simply by protests, violence, conflict, or official staged proceedings, such as arrests, arraignments, meetings, trials, sentencings, or press conferences.

Journalists need to report comprehensively on whatever might be said to exist as objective reality or truth. Beyond those things on which most, or many, reasonable people can agree (the Bulls beat the Rams, or the school board met and recommended a 22 percent increase in the library budget, for example), journalists should solicit as many perspectives as possible and spend as much time involving as many sources and discussants as they can.

Reporters, editors, and probably millions in the public might object, arguing that the result of such coverage is not news. It may be a good magazine piece or something for a book, but it is not for the newspaper. In fact, this is *not* news as we know it. However, a central argument of this book is that news as we know it does not work well because it does not, by and large, help improve the quality of public discourse. Television and radio focus on timeliness and transitory events, and given the nature of those media, they are well suited to do so. Newspapers traditionally focused on the same things, but as competition with other media intensified, they explored other kinds of information and avenues of presenting it. Many of these efforts have been frivolous. Newspapers and other written media can explore alternative ways of sharing information with the public. In so doing, they will not negate criticism or make it unnecessary, but they will enable people to participate better in their own communities and give them a more active role in determining their own fates.

Since the problem of fact and truth remains unresolved, how journalists perceive the result of their work determines what becomes news. As Romano (1987, p. 42) noted, "Nothing in the nature or meaning of 'news' and 'facts' requires the press to cover what it does." Many journalists see what they do as reflecting reality rather than offering stories and information that serve particular interests or purposes. To see news as coherent narratives rather than mirror images of truths or realities would, as Romano suggested, provide more flexibility and allow for different, and probably better, news.

Objectivity is not obsolete; in fact, our major argument is not with objectivity in its connotation of fairness, but with objectification and nonengagement. News seems sterile and meaningless to many people, in part because of the routines, rituals, and contents and forms that are made necessary by strict adherence to traditional notions of objectivity. This adherence leads to a news driven by objective realities in a world driven by selective perceptions and other human qualities that encourage multiple realities. The artificial balancing of extreme positions that masquerades as objectivity in U.S. news is more likely to polarize and entrench opinion rather than encourage discussion. Such an objectivity turns news events into objects and commodities, making them and the news they engender distant and disengaged.

News formats that honor only entrenched opinion ultimately discourage participation and create an audience of consumers. A lively, involved news that both encourages and provokes participation is not likely to be viewed as objective. This does not mean devaluing fairness, but it means that journalists must experiment with approaches, activities, and perspectives that result in stories and articles that engage readers, bringing them into the conversation of news.

THE COMMODITY CRITIQUE: ALL THE NEWS THAT'S EASY TO PRINT

Critics attack the capitalistic nature of news frequently and on several fronts. Entman (1989) observed that economics "shapes the values that guide the creation of news—brevity, simplicity, predictability, timeliness" (p. 19). Short, simple, predictable, and timely articles have proved cheap, efficient, easy to produce, and popular, leaving their creators with little incentive to do anything different. Given increased chain ownership and larger media conglomerates, along with uncertain economic times for various media, including newspapers that face competitive pressures from emerging and newly defined electronic media, the focus on economics and bottom-line management seems now to be a permanent part of journalism.

That news is a commodity is hardly debatable. Early American newspapers published articles about all kinds of things, but for the most part emphasized opinion. Through the middle 1800s or so, partisan papers enthusiastically supported their own political agendas and vigorously and even viciously attacked those of their opponents. The papers focused political issues and tenaciously clung to their own views while hammering the opposition. This preaching to the converted limited the potential for vastly increased circulations.

When publishers fully realized the economic potential of newspapers reaching vast numbers of people, advertising became the primary means of income, and newspapers redefined articles, by practice, at least, as commodities that must be sold to ever-increasing numbers of people. Before commercialization, news seemed dedicated to inform, incite, stimulate, and move people to do something or think some way—to influence. After the commercialization of news, its purposes seemed to narrow to gratification and appeasement. News creators concentrated on topics that large numbers of people might enjoy or be fascinated by, including much of what papers offer today—crime, sex, sports, financial news, and "human interest," a vaguely defined concept that includes everything from highly charged accounts of abused children to cute briefs on the exploits of heroic pets.

Critics such as Postman (1985) have charged that news media, as well as education and religion, stress entertainment too much as a dominant function. Many newspapers increased this emphasis at the same time that talk, reality, and magazine-type, pseudo-news shows multiplied and flourished on television and radio. Local and national network newscasts often feature entertainment-oriented pieces, and the cult of celebrity seems to have sharply increased its members. "Entertainment" spawned "infotainment" as documentary begat "docudrama" and "information" begat "infomercial," all of which signaled the blurring of fact, fiction, information and entertainment or, to some, the real and the fake. Boorstin

(1961) foresaw these kinds of metamorphoses when he wrote about pseudo-events and the gradual overcoming of substance by shadow.

Criticism of this "blurring" often focuses on television, but most of us can name several prominent events, including Janet Cooke's fabricated *Washington Post* story about Jimmy, the child drug addict, or *USA Today*'s misused photos of gun-toting gang members, to show that newspapers are not immune to contrived, entertainment-driven stories and images. Still, newspaper readership is at best flat; thus, many news executives accepted the notion that entertainment increases people's interest and so provided more entertainment, chiefly by expanding "lifestyle," "entertainment," and other so-called "nonnews" sections of the paper.

The blurring of news and entertainment is most evident in sensational coverage of crime, sex, and natural disasters. The term "sensational" is thrown around frequently, especially when violence or crime dominates news coverage, as the beating by Los Angeles police of Rodney King, the rioting that followed the acquittal of four police officers accused in that beating, or the rape trial of William Kennedy Smith in Florida. (Critics complain of excessive and exaggerated coverage, a reasonable complaint given the nature of the events.) Accounts of massive natural disasters, such as an earthquake in San Francisco or the onslaught of Hurricane Andrew in southern Florida and Louisiana, also stimulated such complaints as their coverage lingered in the news for weeks and even months.

Newspapers and newscasts, however, often focus on far more trivial events of disorder, sex, violence, and crime that leave them more vulnerable to charges of sensationalism, illustrating their attempts to provide "news" that is entertaining as well as inexpensive. Newspapers, particularly in medium-sized and smaller metropolitan areas, often emphasize murders, rapes, kidnapping, carjackings, robberies, suicides, and other individual crimes tinged with violence, sex, or oddity. Editors defend extensive use of these articles as giving people what they want, as reflecting what's happening in the community, or as a warning to citizens.

News outlets have little economic incentive to examine crime differently by deemphasizing the individual acts and exploring the roots of crime in a community. Interpretive articles might be less interesting without gruesome, graphic, titillating detail and are more expensive to produce because they require time and experienced, specialized, or more educated reporters. Emphasizing entertainment, whether in features or crime and violence, is generally cheaper and easier than involving people as part of the news through engaging stories of context and perspective. One approach provides entertainment, the other engagement; one is for the consumer, the other for the citizen.

A news-as-commodity approach conforms as well to traditional content and forms that are based in the capitalistic system. Once publishers realized higher revenues came from advertising rather than from news, they sought audiences to sell to advertisers, which, in turn, created a need for larger quantities of interesting news and information. To extend profits, meet daily deadlines, and guarantee interest, news and information had to be not only compelling but easily and inexpensively obtained. Evolving strategies for news "gathering" met these needs remarkably well, and most journalists of the late 1800s would recognize them in today's newspapers. Reporters were assigned to strategic areas or topics called beats. Police, courts, schools, various government agencies and bureaucracies, legislatures, and local and state governments contained the "news" within quite specific boundaries, almost as if news grew in cultivated, defined fields for harvesting. The metaphor of gathering became pervasive in the modern era.

As the beat system evolved, reporters and their sources—usually officials and various authorities—developed relationships in which each fed off, helped, needed, and used the other. Sources, attempting to control and manage information, recognized their favored positions and hired liaisons between themselves and the press. These developments provided even more cheap and ready information to reporters at the same time that they gave sources more, but by no means total, control over the kinds of information that became available to reporters.

Naturally, savvy reporters discovered news by other means and used information provided by press agents in various, and not always flattering ways. However, as functionaries within increasingly complex and profit-oriented bureaucracies, they did what was necessary to get as much information as efficiently as possible. Newsrooms streamlined and routinized reporting, editing, and printing activities, under pressure from daily deadlines.

Form in journalism has been at least as oppressive as content. Darnton (1975) reminded us, in his memoir about his days at the *New York Times*, that reporters often rely on widely used and even ancient story forms. Eventually, journalists honed form down to the simple, efficient *inverted pyramid*, an ordering of information from most to least significant, which dictates content by limiting not only how articles are written but also what subjects are reported. Readers, and perhaps journalists as well, in part define news through its inverted pyramid mold. Publishers of supermarket tabloids often put even their most outrageous articles in inverted pyramid format (Bird, 1992), making them more credible, perhaps, and lampooning the seriousness that people accord to news accounts. An account of a school board meeting, for example, when written as a review or an essay, may not be seen as "news" in the same sense as a school board article written in traditional journalistic style, even though they provide the same information.

The inverted pyramid and its pervasive acceptance defines, in effect, what is reportable and models a worldview that is essentially positivist in philosophy and naively modernist. The inverted pyramid model presumes that human stories are not webs of significance with multiple interconnected causes and effects but are instead linear sequences of acts and events in which it is possible, through diligent investigation, to know and uncover the single most important fact or set of facts, irrespective of audience or context. If they spotlight and isolate that fact, some reporters believe, the rest of the article will largely write itself. However, some of our most critically important human stories are so culturally embedded (e.g., racism, homophobia) or so incrementally slow to develop (e.g., the deterioration of road and bridge infrastructure, an increasingly unstable natural ecology, or changing public attitudes about libraries) that they do not fit as news stories until a crisis—a riot, bridge collapse, or censorship flap—recognizably jumps to the foreground of our consciousness. In other words, the inverted pyramid model subtly presumes that journalists will tell primarily those stories that are easiest to tell—the stories of the surface, the events of entertainment or fear. The hardest stories to talk about, and the ones for which we need journalists the most, remain too deep for the inverted pyramid model to probe.

The model proved economical, however, for gathering, presenting, and reading simplistic news, and it remains economical in several important respects. Reporters at various stages of training use it to write efficiently about specialized topics without any particular expertise in them. Consistency of form makes it easier for reporters to reach quick judgments of newsworthiness, which means that issues and events that easily fit into the form more often become news. Furthermore, the form reduces the burdens of writing. With the form of virtually every kind of article preset, reporters can think more about wording and style, though in time, those also tend to become routine. Because the least important information is at the bottom of the article, editors find the inverted pyramid easy to edit. Shortening often requires no more than trimming from the bottom, a procedure that is less advisable with other narrative forms, such as cautionary tales or jokes, where important information is more likely to be at the bottom than at the top of a story. Finally, readers have grown accustomed to getting important information quickly, thereby making it unnecessary to read beyond the first couple of paragraphs.

The inverted pyramid essentially made it easier for journalists on deadline to select information that made sense out of a complex and chaotic world. As journalism developed, the need for fairness and responsibility increased. To mollify critics, meet emerging journalistic standards, and appeal to the broadest possible public, journalists developed strategies, routines, and procedures for a fair and responsible news, further reinforcing the efficiency of the inverted pyramid form, which was convenient, perhaps even ideal, for presenting stripped down facts with little apparent interpretation or personal stain. Accurately quoting authoritative, and often official, sources on "both sides" of an issue effectively still meets the guidelines for complete, fair reporting. Newspapers and reporters are less likely to be blamed for these so-called objective articles, in which acusations, assertions, and controversial comments are attributed to the proper sources.

Articles about complex issues frequently became articles about people deemed as leaders who offer supporting or opposing viewpoints on those issues, simplifying them and meeting the editors' insistence that the news be "humanized." News often reduces enormously complex issues to conflicts between politicians or other people the news elevates to celebrity status or anoints as important enough to be quoted. Otherwise, the news is peopled with "sources," who again are usually authoritative and official but are usually unrecognizable as human beings. Essentially interchangeable, news sources are valued for their titles, position, expertise, or known views, but not for any unique character they might have as people.

News content results from economic decisions as much as from any decisions based on what people need to participate in a democratic process. However, even a notion of "what people need" can be argued from an economic perspective. Critics put many spins on the issue of the public's need for news. Those who favor giving people what they want might argue that people are smart and know what they need, and that they communicate that to news organizations through ratings, circulation figures, and other feedback, including letters and phone calls. They say it is presumptuous of journalists to think they know what people need and to force-feed them news that they do not want or cannot use. Giving people what they want solves several problems—it eliminates the dilemma of deciding what people need, clears the way for relatively inexpensive information such as police reports and trial proceedings, and enhances news as a product that people will buy, thereby enhancing the news outlet as a source of advertising.

Giving people what they need to function as collaborative citizens within the public sphere is altogether different, in part because answers do not come from simply inquiring about needs; or, when answers do come, they are open to question. Who decides what people need? McManus (1992) used the terms *economic* and *journalistic* to label models of news, and the kinds of news that encompass what many would assume people "need" fall under the journalistic model. The models exist in tension with each other. An economic approach tends to maximize profit while a journalistic approach tends to maximize public understanding. Both models can be seen at most news outlets, and editors consider many issues and events from both journalistic and economic perspectives. As McManus pointed out, investigative reporting, extensive community surveillance, and most reporting that engages people in the community are expensive, taking up the best reporters and often inordinate amounts of time. Obviously, relying on other agencies, whether wire services, police, courts, or public relations people, is a much less expensive way to accumulate information.

Articles produced by a journalistic model often tend to be future-oriented and complex, and not necessarily tied to such traditional news values of efficiency as timeliness and human interest. They require greater investments of time and energy from news organizations and readers alike, and their rewards are rarely immediate. This is often the kind of news used as examples of what people need—how school board politics influences decisions, why city tax increases have produced both failures and successes in service programs, and how people cope with financial or other kinds of adversity. These articles require tracing money, people, and institutions through tangled trails of contradiction, certainty, vagueness, truth, lies, deceit, heroism, confidence, collusion, and complexity. They require talking and listening to many people.

They also require decent, sensitive reporters and writers, unintimidated by dealing closely with the public, and who can start public conversations about how and why things work, not just tell us that they are broken. A conversation of journalism requires engaging stories from journalists knowledgeable and skilled enough to interpret and provide perspective and context.

McManus noted that people often find serious articles dull or unpopular, perhaps because many tend to be lengthy and to conform to staid journalistic conventions and traditions (making them dull) or because they challenge conventional wisdom, quick-fix solutions, values, prejudices, policies, or leaders (making them unpopular). From an economic point of view, it is an easy decision about what to do with supposedly dull, unpopular, expensive news—discard it in favor of more exciting, popular, and, not accidentally, less expensive news.

A news organization that provides dull and unpopular news will, in a capitalistic system, fail—even if it is efficiently dull. A news organization that engages the public, brings people into conversations, presents a broad range of news, helps them find a perspective, and makes an effort to discuss news in forms that encourage public response and participation is less likely to fail—even if it treats serious issues seriously.

Such an organization should also be less susceptible to the influences of advertisers on content. Newspapers weakened by recession in the late 1980s and early 1990s were seen as vulnerable, and journalism reviews reported horror stories about the press caving in to car dealers, for example. Some papers have automotive sections written by the advertising department to pacify car dealer advertisers offended by articles describing how to buy an automobile wisely, evaluating performance of new cars as poor, or even reporting slumping automobile sales.

The influence of advertisers on news is frequently debated. Car dealers who threaten to pull advertising if the paper publishes certain types of articles clearly attempt to influence editorial content. The attempt is successful when papers publish apologies where none is justified, provide free space in "advertorial" sections, monitor their news for information dealers might find offensive, or publish largely positive articles about dealerships, their cars, services, or personnel. Perhaps the most insidious threat to editorial integrity comes when news outlets modify news or kill article ideas because they involve large advertisers.

These practices may be in critics' minds as much as in the day-to-day working world of media news but that they exist at all damages the integrity of journalism. Short of drastically changing the way media make money—that is, abolishing advertising as the major source of revenues—these kinds of influences, or the threat or perception of them, will always exist. Rather than shrink, advertising seems to grow. Some outlets ostensibly free of advertising, such as the Public Broadcasting System or local "community radio" stations, are slowly coming to resemble commercial outlets as their recognition of sponsors and benefactors increasingly look and sound like commercials. Furthermore, the "total management concept" strategies embraced by some newsrooms encourages closer working relationships among the various departments, including news and advertising, which traditionally had little communication.

In short, we see little evidence that news can be free from advertising influences or that news outlets will become less dependent on advertising. In fact, advertising is likely to move into many more areas of our lives. Therefore, to maintain relative independence from advertising influences, journalism should solidify its relationships with the people, for it is ultimately the people, and not advertisers, who provide a news outlet's reason for being and source of power.

One way to build public confidence and trust is to bring economics openly into the conversation. Does advertising affect news? People have their own suspicions and hopes and will share them. Academic researchers have studied the question for decades and published stacks of articles and books on it. Editors, publishers, producers, reporters, and advertisers all have ideas. Advertising influence has been an important question in schools; why should it not be in the news?

NEWS: TOWARD PARTICIPATION AND CONVERSATION

News alone, as we have seen, has no exact, universally accepted meaning. A newspaper article in Taipei will mean something entirely different than an article with the same content in Tacoma. As part of a social and cultural environment, news derives meaning from that environment and its people. News is not gathered and distributed but created and shared; therefore, writers and readers, as part of a particular society and culture, contribute to its meaning. To paraphrase Hartley (1982), news does not originate meanings as much as it reproduces or reflects dominant meanings.

Even though news reinforces the power by which the powerful obtain and maintain influence, Hartley argued that news is more than propaganda for the power structure. Propaganda is contestable; news is not. Media content, as it is casual, often serendipitous, cumulative, and based on common sense, develops like conversation. In the sense that and to the degree which news inhabits a framework of common sense—recognized, accepted, and shared without a lot of reasoning, thought, or analysis—it is, Hartley thought, seen as natural and therefore incontestable.

Rachlin (1988) argued that the perception that media provide objective information gives them status and power, particularly because they package a particular worldview, which both he and Hartley say is perceived as natural. The media project this view, which is in part generated through media practices, conventions, routines, rituals, and traditions, throughout their content and form. In so doing, they inculcate hegemonic values and attitudes by "simple repetitive exposure, rather than considered judgment" (Rachlin, 1988, p. 25). Some argue that the diffusion of a consistent set of values and attitudes decreases or contains conflict, effectively preventing challenges to "the way things are," thereby reinforcing them as natural and incontestable.

European scholars, including Hall (1975, 1977, 1984), Hall and colleagues (1981), Hartley (1982), and van Dijk (1988), have been more inclined than scholars from the United States to critique hegemony and ideology in the news. Van Dijk, for example, found that news reports not only provide the general outline of "social, political, cultural, and economic models of societal events" but also adopt frameworks that make the models intelligible (p. 182). This, he argued, discourages people from developing knowledge and attitudes that lead to alternative frameworks. If news provides a dominant interpretation of events, then people dependent on news for much of what they know about the world are likely to accept that interpretation as "correct" and are less likely to understand the necessity of dialogue with opposing or different perspectives.

Two U.S. media critics arguing along similar lines, Chomsky (1989) and Herman (1992), claimed that the U.S. press reflects values and ideologies of government by consistently supporting the party line or, as Herman more colorfully asserted, consistently swallowing government propaganda. Blatantly political, these critics often seem more disenchanted with society than media, though they may argue that media cannot be seen as separate from the society in which they reside. In fact, for Jensen (1990) virtually any criticism of mass media is a critique of modern society. Chomsky and Herman explore the stifling of dissent through two themes: media news acquiescence to official government versions of events and interpretations of issues and inaccessibility of media news to all but the rich and powerful.

In a less ideological critique, Bennett (1988) said that "advertisements for authority" dominate news, which is otherwise filled with articles of violence, disorder, economic and social insecurity, deviance, cultural erosion, and threats of war, all of which "reinforce public support for political authorities who promise order, security, and responsive political solutions" (xii).

News, Bennett argued, is not fit for democracy because it is "superficial, narrow, stereotypical, propaganda-laden, of little explanatory value, and not geared for critical debate or citizen action" (p. 9). News does not advance the cause of democracy, he says, because it *personalizes* (gives preference to individual actors over institutional or political considerations), *dramatizes* (emphasizes crisis over continuity and personal drama over persistent problems of our time), *fragments* (comes in self-contained capsules without context), and *normalizes* (assures that officials acting in our interest will return things to normal).

Bennett argued that people do not receive enough critical information from the press to make informed decisions, thereby decreasing their psychic and behavioral participation in the democratic process. As participation decreases, people are less likely to perceive the need for or request critical information. News media perpetuate the cycle. In so doing, they discourage people from being reflective about their communities and their own lives.

The most prominent academic approach to the study of news has been the sociological, which usually stresses creation of news and organizational forces or routines. These shed light on some variables of publishing and broadcasting, but rarely do more than describe. Some influences on the creation of news include gate-keepers (White, 1964); socialization (Breed, 1955; Molotch & Lester, 1974); the nature of story (Darnton, 1975; Hughes, 1968); processes, routines, and rituals (Tuchman, 1972, 1978; Fishman, 1980; Roshco, 1975; Epstein, 1974); values (Gans, 1979); and conventions (Schiller, 1981).

News is more than its practice, its form or content; it is more than information, fact, or entertainment. Media abhor a vacuum, and as they spread to fill every empty space, they make it impossible to live in the world and escape their content and influence. As we liberalize our notions of definitions and venues of news, suggesting, for example, that "new news" comes from movies, rap songs, talk shows, computer networks, and other sources (as compared with "old news" from packaged mainstream news sources such as newspapers), news becomes more culturally significant and understanding it in a larger context more relevant. Because of the ephemeral and often superficial nature of the culture-driven "new news," however, we must strengthen the emphasis of mainstream journalism on stimulating thorough discussion and deliberation.

Many of these arguments about news influences, both ideological and sociological, contradict the conventional wisdom about journalism, particularly that in which the press claims to be free and have an adversarial relationship with government. Freedom of the press is relative, and no doubt the U.S. press has more technical freedoms than most. But those freedoms operate within parameters limited by many considerations, including: adherence to the journalistic ideal of objectivity; more or less rigid journalistic forms; dependence on official sources, press releases, "pseudo-events," and beat systems (in which specific topics or areas are systematically covered); traditional definitions and attributes of news; journalists' perceptions and ideological learnings; and resistance to change other than technological. Journalists also operate within many other boundaries: libel, copyright, and other laws; codes of ethics and internal guidelines; pressures from special-interest groups, critics, and peers in the newsrooms; and economic pressures from corporate owners and advertisers.

Empirical scholars and researchers have attempted to measure these influences but have provided, as we might guess, little hard evidence of precise effects. Instead, they have shown clearly that the media operate in a system of enormous complexity that defies linear cause-effect models and explanations. Comparatively free, our news media nonetheless operate under restraints that for whatever reasons result in a news that reflects society's authority structure. A vast number of citizens thus become invisible, and then, functionally powerless.

In the early 1990s, at a peak of U.S. antitax, antispending sentiment, several events highlighted the influence of talk shows and other participative media formats. When Congress attempted to increase salaries, Washington was flooded with letters and calls originating from radio talk show discussions. In the 1992 presidential election, third party candidate H. Ross Perot bought thirty-minute blocks of commercial time on network television stations and toured TV and radio talk shows, essentially skirting the traditional press. Journalists criticized Perot's and Bill Clinton's decisions to submit to fewer traditional interviews in favor of appearances with more direct audience contact. Rather than agree with this press condemnation, the public appeared to welcome and encourage the candidates' tactics. At the same time, even tradition-bound newspapers instituted programs designed to increase the people's involvement in news operations (Rosen, 1991a).

The previous few years had already seen cataclysmic events, including the tearing down of the Berlin Wall, the collapse of Soviet communism, bloody protests for democracy in Communist China, diminished white rule in Africa, the Gulf War, and the creation of new democratic republics in Eastern Europe and else-where. Images of freedom and people fighting and dying for freedom filled American mass media for several years. In this context, changes occurred in the United States, too. *Rolling Stone* writer Jon Katz (1992) and others argued, essentially, that people had finally taken matters into their own hands and, armed with talk shows and other interactive media, particularly computers, they had changed the nature of news. The more extreme of these observers believed that the arrogant press and its tradition of delivering the Truth from official sources on high to a thankful and passive audience was shaken. People sampled participation, they liked it, and they had the means to break free from a press that had ignored them too long. This interpretation may or may not prove to be valid, but certainly the mainstream press now has to face the challenge and potential to revitalize its notions of "news" and "audience."

Journalism can broaden its notions of news by bringing more dimensions and perspectives into the conversation, by including a larger spectrum of people in society; news need not be only the official version, and it can explore human affairs as much as government affairs. It can remove bonds and boundaries of objectivity without abandoning fairness as it encourages journalists from various ideological perspectives to use the full range of their abilities to converse with the full range of their audiences. At the same time, we can define those audiences as active, inquiring citizens who have something worth saying about what concerns them and their community. Citizens might consume food, toothpaste, and other products, but they live within news, and it is the responsibility of the journalist to include them in the social and political conversation. After all, who else will?

4

Ecumenical Journalism: The Multicultural and Multidisciplinary Commons

John Calhoun Merrill invited criticism, and even ridicule, with his book *Existential Journalism* (1977). He wanted to inspire a serious discussion of journalism's intellectual roots and concerns but doubted whether the journalism community, including fellow academics, would be receptive. Prior to writing the book, Merrill surveyed journalists and journalism educators, asking: "What meaning do you give to the term 'existential journalism'? Please give main characteristics that come to mind or anything else you would like to say about the term" (p. 25). The professional journalists' responses especially revealed what Merrill described as a "mixture of mystification, irritation, and sarcasm, and—I might add—ignorance" (p. 25). One editor wrote: "We are getting people out of the journalism schools who can't spell, who can't compose a lead and never heard of libel, and you ask me to share your concern about existential journalism. I've never heard of it, I haven't got the time to look it up, and I doubt whether it has anything to do with the real world of writing and editing—or the teaching thereof" (p. 26). The survey responses reinforced Merrill's belief that journalism would rather not engage in serious introspection, preferring to dismiss questions about its philosophical foundation as academic busywork.

Merrill identified and contrasted two basic orientations in journalism: the existentialist and rationalist. The existentialist includes humanistic, informal, emotional, intuitive, subjective, and personal elements within journalism. The rationalist more closely reflects the norms of most "institutionalized" or "establishment" journalism: objective, impersonal, formal, disinterested, and unemotional reportage. The existential journalist, Merrill concluded, values experimentation, diversity, creativity, and pluralism, whereas the rationalist journalist values consistency, sameness, conformity, and monism (pp. 45–46). Most journalists, Merrill wrote, tend to fall into one or the other camp. The existentialist orientation stresses action and involvement, receptivity and sensitivity. Merrill's existential journalism does not promote irrational, reckless, irresponsible behavior. Rather, he saw existentialism as journalism's natural calling—an imaginative, committed journalism that society needs and expects.

The existential orientation encourages journalists to take risks, to be courageous, to consider alternatives to the conventional. Institutionalized journalism, Merrill said, fears and resists the unconventional. Merrill's willingness to question the status quo encouraged us to identify the spirit or attitude that complements his notion of existential journalism. We chose the term *ecumenical journalism*. *Ecumenical* comes from the Greek *oikoumenikos*: of or from the whole world. In a modern sense, *ecumenical* came to mean bringing the "whole inhabited world" (the *oikoumene*) to "its true destiny within the purpose of God" (Goodall, 1972, p. vii). After Pope John XXIII called the Second Vatican Council in 1969, the term gained popularity and significance beyond its initial connection to Christianity, in general, and the Roman Catholic Church, in particular. With its Decree on Ecumenism, the Vatican Council stressed the importance of unity and dialogue within the Christian community, saying that "through such dialogue everyone gains a truer knowledge and more just appreciation of the teaching and religious life of both [all] communions" (Goodall,

1972, p. 128). In the 1970s, ecumenism spread as a movement of Christian churches to promote cooperation and better understanding among different faiths.

A secular application of ecumenism aptly fits journalism as it could be expanded and practiced. We focus primarily on two qualities of ecumenism—its connotation of *universal* or *whole-world inclusiveness* and its emphasis on *heightened understanding and cooperation through dialogue*. The ecumenical movement's inclusiveness—its recognition and embrace of other faiths—parallels journalism's growing attention to diversity in news. Journalists increasingly use terms like "voice" and "community" as they seek ways to become more representative, responsive, and relevant. Rather than stand apart from the community to *preach* the news, journalists now must recognize how communication—two-way, interactive and dialogical, when possible—promotes understanding and cooperation among people and within communities. As ecumenism emphasizes, while we may follow different paths, we are fundamentally united in wanting a society that works, ill-defined and contentious as it sometimes might be. But to find a common ground we must acknowledge and respect our differences.

Ecumenical journalism expands the traditional focus on the "public's right to know," encompassing a broader emphasis—the "public's right to be heard." Despite its proclaimed devotion to the public, including its recent attention to community building, journalism still offers news in the public's name without sufficient concern for public involvement. Conventional journalism appears—and sometimes is—arrogant, because of what it presumes on behalf of those it supposedly serves. Journalists do not pass along all they know, for most withhold or filter ten times as much information as they disseminate. People, presumably, need only what journalists anoint as newsworthy. Practically speaking, journalism defines the extent of the public's right to know. However, if the right to know constitutes a cornerstone of a self-governing, democratic people, knowledge by which to govern ought not be controlled by a few gatekeepers. Instead, that knowledge should be shared widely—and it should be generated through inclusive dialogue.

Ecumenical journalism defies precise definition because it is less a technique or style than an attitude of news that hears diverse voices and perspectives within a context of interpretation and analysis. It recognizes the interconnectedness of social and political forces and it attempts to engage the public in an inclusive public conversation about values and common ground. Journalism's central mission, as we see it, is to stimulate and guide the conversation that helps us recognize what we share, what we value, how we differ, how we are alike. In this sense, the search for "common ground," far from implying agreement or simple consensus, becomes a search for a metaphorical *place for social dialogue*—the ground that becomes "common" is the ground upon which the public's talk occurs. To fulfill its responsibilities, journalism must consider its role as a listener and facilitator, hearing and heeding society's many voices; generating dialogue; contributing to understanding; and helping people and communities live, work, and govern together. Ecumenical journalism necessarily includes various methodologies of news and analysis. Journalism has the responsibility to view the world holistically from different perspectives, becoming multidisciplinary as well as multicultural.

An ecumenical approach does not represent "touchy-feely" New Age sentiment as parodied in a *New York Times* magazine piece (Kelly & Dowd, 1992) published prior to President Clinton's inauguration: "We're in a reaching out sort of mood this Inauguration. We're connecting. We're opening up. We're celebrating diversity and embracing wholeness. We're on an odyssey of self-discovery. We're thinking communitarian, New Covenant, a Government that looks like America, inclusive not exclusive, omnicultural . . ." (p. 20). Why, though, must journalism reward attitudes and behavior—whether in government or journalism—that belittle dialogue and involvement and support monologue, pessimism, and detachment? Increasingly, however, nontraditional themes are being expressed. *Des Moines Register* editor Geneva Overholser (Stein, 1992), for example, urged journalism to pursue news that provides perspective and shows a heart. In a similar vein, Teresa Baggot (1992) cited mounting evidence of a journalism that cares for others, upholds human dignity and promotes the community's well-being. Overholser and Baggot have described a kind of ecumenical journalism.

THE MEANING OF "MULTICULTURAL"

In cities with sizable Latino populations, such as Tampa and Phoenix, a young woman's fifteenth birthday marks her coming of age. If she belongs to a family of means, a *quinceaneras* party often will highlight the occasion. At its most lavish, quinceaneras resembles a debutante ball, with billowy gowns, champagne, and ballroom dancing. For the young women and their families, it is a time of great pride and happiness, yet few Anglo journalists know about the custom in more than a general way. A feature story on quinceaneras promotes multicultural awareness among Anglos; it also conveys a message to Latinos: "We see you; we recognize your distinctiveness; you matter." An ecumenical approach values all humans and, when applied to journalism, recognizes the potential for news in relationships between people. Ecumenical journalism, then, quite naturally becomes multicultural.

Despite our current preoccupation with the word "multiculturalism," we cannot seem to agree on its meaning. Like other members of the "ism" family, multiculturalism suggests dogma and ideology. In one of its many manifestations, multiculturalism rallies socially and politically disenfranchised groups, particularly blacks, gays, and feminists. Leonard Jeffries (Morrow, 1991), for example, has aggressively promoted an Afrocentric perspective in words that shock, offend, and anger many whites and nonwhites alike. Jeffries saw demons in the dominant "Eurocentric culture," and he lashed out against them. Arthur M. Schlesinger Jr.'s *The Disuniting of America* (1992) condemned efforts to promote separatism and Europhobia. When wielded as a weapon in a war of ideology, "multiculturalism" promotes divisiveness, not togetherness. It seems, at times, that multiculturalism's "Hatfields and McCoys" do more harm than good, forgetting, if they ever knew, the reason multiculturalism became an issue of serious concern. It need not be so. Molefi Asante (1992) believes that the term "multiculturalism" in education is basically "self-defining": "It is simply the idea that the educational experience should reflect the diverse cultural heritage of our system of knowledge" (p. 305).

We believe that journalism similarly should define and practice multiculturalism in the middle ground, between the extremes of cultural separatism and monocultural hegemony. There we find the *ideal* of multiculturalism, which supports the view that through heightened sensitivity and increased communication we will come to see and hear one another more clearly, more humanely. What we perceive, of course, will neither preclude conflict nor make agreement easier. The United States is a multicultural society; there is no denying our condition. After all, what alternatives do we have? Festering resentment, hate, violence, isolation, or segregation? We have little choice but to listen to one another, seek understanding, and promote respect for what others legitimately value. It is naive to envision a world in perfect harmony, but it is neither naive nor wasted energy to build toward a realistic multi-culturalism. If multiculturalism in its apolitical sense means sincere attempts to recognize, accept, and respect human differences, then, it seems, progress toward the ideal is possible and well worth the effort.

The news often portrays only shards of a world. In spring 1992, we stared at television screens, watching and rewatching video clips of Korean shopkeepers firing on Latino looters, of young black men pulling a white driver from his truck and beating him senseless, and of ordinary people arguing without listening about sources of injustice. Los Angeles erupted after an all-white jury acquitted the police officers accused of beating Rodney King, an African-American. The first Rodney King verdict (two officers later were convicted on federal charges) provided the catalyst; it did not represent the cause, for the cause is complex and perhaps beyond our ability to determine or comprehend. However, we still feel compelled to do something. We see symptoms of a divisiveness and hostility, and we react, as did *Oakland Tribune* writer William Wong (1991), who witnessed an unsettling episode while dining at a restaurant in Oakland's Chinatown. Two African-American men entered and soon grew agitated over perceived delays and affronts by the waiter and the hostess. When the manager told the two to leave, the older man suddenly overturned a table, spilling plates and a tray of condiments. Ugly words were exchanged before the men departed. In a column, Wong observed:

> Other than this being a raw slice of life in the big city, what are we to make of this scene? I do not take it as "typical" of relations between African Americans and Chinese or other people of Asian descent. Every day, I see trouble-free inter-actions among Asian, black, Latino and white people of all endeavors—work, recreation, schools. But I would be naive to think that hateful confrontations haven't occurred or won't again occur with racially charged currents surging to the surface. . . . Complicated and seemingly irreconcilable value differences and stereotypes hang over us. Pieties about a harmonious multicultural future mean nothing to the down-trodden poor or the parochial business owner. (p. C15)

Wong is right to warn that multiculturalism must be more than sloganeering. However, journalists cannot afford to stand above the fray as critics or observers. To remain a vital force for the exchange of ideas in society, journalists and news organizations must become conversational catalysts, bridging multiple com-munities in dialogue that crosses cultures and differences of race, gender, age, and social station.

Journalists cannot claim ecumenism by offering occasional stories about diversity. To respond to the need for diversity in news by article quotas or per capita-dictated representativeness may fulfill requirements but not the spirit of multicultural or dialogic journalism. Stories about ethnic holidays such as Kwanzaa or Cinco de Mayo amount to window dressing for millions of Ameri-cans who find little of relevance in the morning newspaper or the local newscast. Even a prominently featured quinceaneras story, despite good intentions, may strike some Latinos as condescending. Perhaps the article serves as an interesting repast for Anglo curiosity, but to many Latinos, its significance pales compared to an investigative piece on how pesticides endanger migrant workers or how Mexican-American attorneys are increasingly influential in the politics of the Southwest. Latinos or others outside the mainstream require evidence that the news is "theirs," too. Mainstream journalism, long estranged from some segments of the population, must convince the public that its efforts toward representative, equitable coverage are not simply symbolic or token but a genuine sign of cultural awareness and respect.

Simply reporting that the community is comprised of diversity is not difficult; the more challenging task is to unfold the underlying contributions of diversity to public life and to integrate that diversity naturally into the daily news. It is not a matter of injecting more black or brown faces in the news, or showing people in wheelchairs, or covering gay marches. Splashes of "minority" news here or there actually accentuate a far deeper problem. Most of the time, minorities feel the majority culture looks through them, rendering them practically invisible. When minorities are "noticed" in the news, the response seems inappropriate, even offensive, because journalism sometimes treats minorities as information-age welfare recipients—vulnerable souls who need help or protection or, worse, a pat on the head from journalism. Multicultural news cannot succeed if those it purportedly acknowledges view it as an act of noblesse oblige.

A multicultural approach would refocus coverage from its normal emphasis on the values and concerns of upper- or middle-class, mainstream culture to view the community and its people from what Gans (1979) calls a "bottom up" perspective (pp. 313, 320). Gans's unfortunate terminology suggests a preferential socioeconomic hierarchy, but his approach properly encourages journalists to draw upon wider and more diverse attitudes and experiences. To reach into the community means finding ways to *solicit* and *obtain* feedback rather than waiting for letters to an editor or calls to an ombudsperson. Some news organizations hold public forums to sample opinion. This is a step in the right direction, but forums attract people with the time, transportation, and often the vested interests to attend. Journalism needs listening outposts throughout the community, where people gather and live.

Ecumenical journalism *merges* and represents the multicultural diversity of people and viewpoints without *submerging* them, so that through conversation and compromise, problems can be identified and solutions genuinely tried.

JOURNALISM'S ECUMENICAL RESPONSIBILITY

In the soul-searching that followed the Los Angeles riots, Professor Cornel West (1992) urged that we begin to reset our fractured society by acknowledging the basic humanness we share: "We must acknowledge that as a people—*E Pluribus Unum*—we are on a slippery slope toward economic strife, social turmoil and cultural chaos. If we go down, we go down together. The Los Angeles upheaval forced us to see not only that we are not connected in ways we would like to be but also, in a more profound sense, that this failure to connect binds us even more tightly together. The paradox of race in America is that our common destiny is more pronounced and imperiled precisely when our divisions are deeper" (p. 25). West expressed a major social theme for the 1990s—the search for our common stake in community and for the kinds of communication that enable it. That theme resonates in many ways with two important books about ourselves and our environment—*Habits of the Heart* (1986) and its sequel, *The Good Society* (1991), by sociologist Robert Bellah and his colleagues. Bellah and West similarly attempted to reconcile humankind's differences with our commonalities, such as concerns for social and economic justice, freedom in its various forms, self-fulfillment, and community advancement. We exist in a fragile, cultural ecosystem that must be preserved and protected. In other words, we must know about, care about, and care for each other if we are to survive as a society, much less prosper. Above all, perhaps, from the perspective of journalism, we need access to each other to speak, to be heard, and to hear.

If it chooses, journalism can help society move beyond mere expressions of *tolerance* for differences to reach a higher ground of appreciation for and promotion of our diversity. From there, conversation can begin. Others have marked the path in persuasive, prophetic language: Judge Learned Hand in 1943, the Hutchins Commission in 1947, and the Kerner Commission in 1968.

Journalism, said Judge Hand (*United States v. Associated Press*, 1943), "serves one of the most vital of all general interests: the dissemination of news from many different sources, with as many different facets and colors as is possible. That interest is closely akin to, if indeed it is not the same as, the interest protected by the First Amendment; it presupposes that right conclusions are more likely to be gathered out of a multitude of tongues than any kind of authoritative selection." Judge Hand's opinion springs from John Milton's 1644 attack against English censorship, *Areopagitica*. In poetic language, Milton championed diversity in communication. "[H]ow can we more safely, and with less danger, scout into the regions of sin and falsity than by reading all manner of tractates and hearing all manner of reason?" he asked.

The 1947 "Hutchins Report" (Leigh, 1974), *A Free and Responsible Press*, expressed concern that concentrated media ownership and power limited the variety of sources of news and opinion, and it called for the press to project a "representative picture of the constituent groups in the society." It encouraged the news media to portray the country's diversity—"its various values, its aspirations, and its common humanity," adding the observation: "If people are exposed to the inner truth of the life of a particular group, they will gradually build up respect for and understanding of it" (p. 27).

Twenty years later, after America's cities erupted in rioting, the Kerner Report (1968) blamed news media for failing to report adequately on society's underlying racial problems. In pointed words that have echoed into the 1990s, the report criticized the news media for not telling the whole story:

> [The news media] have not communicated to the majority of their audience—which is white—a sense of degradation, misery, and hopelessness of living in the ghetto. They have not communicated to whites a feeling for the difficulties and frustrations of being a Negro in the United States. They have not shown understanding and appreciation of—and thus have not communicated—a sense of Negro culture, thought, or history. . . . By failing to portray the Negro as a matter of routine and in the context of the total society, the news media have, we believe, contributed to the black-white schism in this country (p. 383). . . . To editors who say we have run thousands of inches on the ghetto which nobody read and to television executives who bemoan scores of underwatched documentaries, we say: find more ways of telling this story, for it is a story you, as journalists, must tell—honestly, realistically, and imaginatively. . . . With notable exceptions, the media have not yet turned to the task with the wisdom, sensitivity, and expertise it demands. (p. 384)

Today, while journalism reflects on such warnings and advice, it faces new challenges of providing representative and enlightened news and opinion—challenges that go beyond sensitive writing about diversity. The conflict and division of the 1990s suggest that the healing marketplace of diversity promoted by Judge Hand and the Hutchins and Kerner reports remains more imagined than real.

Can mainstream journalism create a truly public forum? To a degree, the structure of such a forum already exists in tradition and practice. The history of American journalism shows how media have addressed a remarkable array of issues and problems, and editorial commentary has contributed context and interpretation from a variety of political and social perspectives. Mainstream journalism need only structure a larger, more inviting, and more inclusive forum, sharing its control of news and opinion with its diverse community. It is in its role of expanding the public conversation that mainstream journalism can outperform the alternative news media, which serve relatively narrow audiences and address a relatively narrow range of civic concerns. Mainstream media, with their communicative potential and resources, hold the key to a conversational society.

MULTICULTURALISM IN PRACTICE

To their credit, today's reporters and editors have become vastly more aware of other cultures and perspectives, but they continue to seek news in familiar places and from familiar sources, often overlooking stories outside their predominantly white, middle-class experiences and lives. Understandably, mainstream media struggle to engage a younger, culturally diverse audience now being reached by less conventional outlets of news, information and entertainment. Jon Katz (1992) of *Rolling Stone* pointed to the presidential campaign of 1992 as a watershed event because it signaled the emergence of the "new news" as an energetic, creative and responsive rival to "old news." New news features involving formats—talk shows, call-in programs, music videos, movies— that stimulate dialogue. It is created by people who communicate with passion or humor about public events that touch lives. Old news—represented by metro newspapers, news magazines, and network news —comes to ordinary persons and is "pronounced" or "proclaimed" from distant institutions and officials; feedback and dialogue occur, but not as directly or, it appears, passionately as is possible in the vehicles of new news. In its most remembered slogans—Walter Cronkite's "And that's the way it is" and, from the *New York Times*, "All the News That's Fit to Print"—old news projects an exclusive, officious image.

Katz (1992) predicted a continuing "collison of these old and new media cultures—more and more separated from each other along age, racial, cultural and class lines" (p. 30). *Newsweek*'s Meg Greenfield (1992), trying to explain why journalists misjudge events or get caught off guard, blamed the "impaired ability" of journalists "to understand what others are feeling and thinking, to understand why they behave the way they do, what their lives are like, what their interests are, how things that matter appear to them" (p. 88).

What can we conclude from such observations? Obviously some journalists are closer—in body and spirit—to the extended community and its diversity than others. Journalists, by nature, are not cold, indifferent, or aloof. However, the conditions and rules of their work discourage intimacy. The manufacture of stories often comes first, and many reporters work under production deadlines and quotas. With an eye on the clock, it is difficult to see or hear more than caricatures of people. Journalistic objectivity, usually defined in terms of detachment and noninvolvement, further isolates reporters and editors from people and leads to the objectification of news "subjects," "sources," and "consumers." The competitive pursuit of news motivates journalists to move quickly, aggressively, and dispassionately. The system seldom rewards or encourages patience, sensitivity, and compassion—qualities important to building relationships, achieving understanding, and encouraging communication. Without the time or encouragement, journalists see and hear little outside their cultural and occupational confines.

Multicultural success in journalism depends on a series of introspective steps. The first requires an acknowledgment of the power of the dominant culture. Whites do not readily see themselves as "dominant" or "powerful," since they (we) often overtly subscribe to egalitarianism in professional and social roles. All of us, however, might carefully consider the daily advantages of just one aspect of that power—white privilege—as described by educator Peggy McIntosh (1992): "I can go shopping alone most of the time, pretty well assured that I will not be followed or harassed. If I should need to move, I can be pretty sure of renting or purchasing housing in an area that I can afford and in which I would want to live. I can be pretty sure that my neighbors in such a location will be neutral or pleasant to me" (p. 34). White privilege, if left unchallenged, insulates people and distorts their views of even the most "simple" conditions of everyday life, like renting an apartment or shopping at the mall. For minorities, there is nothing simple about survival in an often hostile environment.

White heterosexual males, in particular, can be oblivious to the cultural realities that surround them. They look superficially at a black, or gay, or female colleague, and they may see a similarity of role and a surface cohesiveness. Since values and rewards in news and in life are based primarily on a white, male, middle-class perception of the social norm, minorities discover that the "white way is the right way," and many adapt constantly in working with or around whites. Outsiders who must operate within a white, male world often don a socially acceptable identity at work or in social affairs to blend in or move ahead. Nonetheless, nonwhite minorities and women, in particular, can feel ignored and devalued. Some, of course, submit to the dominant culture; they suffer—or brood—in silence, but others, in frustration and anger, shout and provoke, hoping to be acknowledged; they, in turn, may find themselves written off by the dominant culture as "militants" or "radicals."

Recognizing the significance of membership in the dominant culture helps journalists take the next step: viewing the world through the eyes of others. William F. Woo (1991), the Asian-American editor of the *St. Louis Post-Dispatch*, reinforced that message: "We do not learn sensitivity in a vacuum, but in trying desperately to get through situations that are pure hell without it. We cannot adequately reproduce the passions of others without an awareness of rage, despair and love in our own lives. We cannot convey success or failure if we pretend that these experiences are remote from us. We cannot understand what people in business or government or the streets are thinking unless we have some informed appreciation for what they go through, day after day" (p. B1). Life can be a series of daily indignities—a secretary who cannot go through a day without enduring sexual innuendos from male workers; a gay server in a restaurant who constantly over-hears customers snickering about "faggots" and macabre AIDS jokes; a black executive who knows that whenever he drives his luxury car he faces being pulled over by police for a "routine" traffic check.

Some would argue the white male mentality precludes the possibility of multicultural understanding. As a popular saying put it: "It's a black thing. You wouldn't understand." Other groups outside the mainstream adopted the message in a display of solidarity based on accumulated frustration and anger from dealing with employers or institutions that so frequently displayed cultural insensitivity, ignorance or, worst of all, indifference. Understandably, minorities may doubt the motives of white males who profess a commitment to multiculturalism. In some cases, doubts and suspicions may persist until genuine, tangible empathy is evident. Empathy describes a sincere attempt to identify with the experiences, emotions, and values of others; it does not necessarily imply agreement, but it does communicate a willingness and an effort to understand.

What must we look for? Through whose eyes should journalists see the world? The "cultures" in "multiculturalism" include, of course, different races and ethnic groups. But we prefer to define "culture" broadly to embrace family, class, gender, sexual orientation, ideological, physical, mental, and generational distinctions and concerns. Working from that expanded definition, journalism can move to multicultural reporting, producing stories and commentary that challenge stereotypes; promote understanding of our differences; celebrate cultural heritage; provide diversity of perspectives on events and issues; and, ultimately, help seemingly ordinary citizens more effectively communicate the extraordinariness of their lives.

Questioning Stereotypes and Biases

In communities across America, people gather under the shade of a sprawling maple or oak, carrying on the tree-gathering, a tradition rooted in African culture. In many African countries, selected trees serve as an oasis, where the elders converse and dispense wisdom and advice. In its transplanted form, a tree-gathering resembles an outdoor social club that values tradition. Reporter Peggy Peterman (1992) described the fellowship and good will of tree-gatherings in St. Petersburg, telling about the friendly sharing of food, conversation, and emotional support. To the culturally uninformed, an outdoor congregation of blacks might be misunderstood. "What's going on? What are they planning? Why are they hanging out like that? Don't they have jobs? They're probably up to no good." Peterman's story about gathering under the trees provided a cultural perspective and taught lessons about seeing and understanding. It represents multicultural reporting because it counteracted "cliches of vision." The story illuminated values and enriched us; it told about an existence far removed from that of most journalists and their audiences; and it gave wholly different meaning to our perceived reality. Multicultural reporting corrects false public impressions, created, in part, by news accounts that present incomplete, distorted pictures of reality.

Before journalists can effectively provide social accounts with cultural dimensions, they should inventory and evaluate personal evidence of their own distorted images, false impressions, latent feelings, and indifference to the plight of others. There must be a willingness to look into a mirror and accept what is revealed. Ask yourself, for example, whether the Reverend Jerry Falwell defines your view of religious fundamentalism. Do you believe, if white, that young, black, inner city males would rather steal than work? Do you believe, if black, that all whites are racist? Do you believe, if male, that women are less rational and more emotional than men, or, whether male or female, do you consider older drivers unsafe? To the extent that humans hold strong beliefs, we become blind or myopic about how and when they shape our actions. Donald Murray (1983) cautioned his colleagues in journalism: "The more professional we become the greater the danger that we will see what we expect to see. Experience, of course, is an advantage, but it has a dark side. It may keep us from seeing the real story: the cause that does not fit the stereotype, the effect that is not predictable, the quote that we do not hear before our question is answered" (p. 29). Murray offered an example of a conditioned, but limiting, newsroom perspective: "There's never a peaceful evening on a Roxbury [urban Boston] street corner where good friends spend a few peaceful hours reminiscing and kidding each other; there's never a Friday evening in a New Hampshire country store marked by distrust, meanness, and potential violence" (p. 31). Avoiding clichés of vision requires an open mind to understand one's own biases and an open heart to understand empathically the attitudes of others.

Offensive stereotypes are not always noticed even when they should be obvious. Consider two examples from the thousands that can be found in newspapers or on newscasts. A California daily, serving a community heavily populated by Asian-Americans, illustrated a story on Japanese cars with a graphic that featured a yellow-colored auto, with a rising sun license plate and slanted headlights for eyes. An apology followed in the next day's newspaper. A Florida newspaper, noted for its efforts at diversity, published a story about fierce opposition to an adult book store, using this analogy to describe the opponents: "like Indians silently lining the cliffs in a wagon train western." An American Indian (Tomas, 1992) told the newspaper the phrase fed stereotypes of the "savage" Indian, waiting to ambush whites—a Hollywood image that many people believe. She added: "Few people have difficulty recognizing racism when it appears in white robes and funny hats. It is much more difficult identifying it in pretty phrases in the newspaper, in so-called clever sports headlines and in the use of offensive terms and names" (p. A13). Neither case represents conscious racism; both come from innocent but hurtful cultural ignorance and insensitivity.

Promoting Understanding

A journalist we know and admire, Reena Shah Stamets (1988), writes about the people of other cultures—old age in Japan, motherhood in India, childhood in a drug-infested American city.

She has explored how different people are, explaining their behavior and reducing the distortion of outsiders' views. Her story
about motherhood in Kenya, for example, explained why many
women in rural areas bear eight, nine, or ten children. Later, she
told a class of journalism students that the women are misunderstood by outsiders, adding "Some journalists parachute in and ask,
'Why do you have so many children?' Let people speak for
themselves without cultural baggage. These are not stupid people;
they aren't just breeding. They make very practical, reasonable
decisions." Her story told of the multiple risks and problems
associated with birth control in a society far removed from suburban America. More important, her story framed a context for a
dialogue about "otherness" that would have been impossible otherwise.

Stamets, who was born in India, knows that communicating in
different settings enhances the experience of entering another
culture. Stamets said that she listens as much for feelings as words,
especially when dealing with languages that might have ten definitions for a single term. For one of her Kenyan stories, she participated in the culture by planting corn with Wanjiru Njuguna
before talking to her about why generations of women of Kenya's
Kikuyu ethnic group work the fields and tend the home while the
men talk politics at the village bar or under a shady tree. Stamets
(1988) wrote: "[A] strange woman from another land is asking her
why a woman should do all this work alone and then rush back
home to light the fire and make dinner. Can't the men in her house
help her? Wanjiru looks at me as though she cannot believe what
I have suggested, but she decides to be patient. For one thing, I am
her guest, and I am also helping her plant the field" (p. 1A).
Stamets's method of "introducing" herself in a culturally acceptable way led to a fruitful discussion of tradition in an African
village, told through stories and talk.

Understanding comes about, too, when we question prevailing
wisdom and doubt contemporary myths. Susan Faludi's book
Backlash (1991) documented case after case of journalists who
uncritically accepted and disseminated reports about the condition

of career-driven, independent women, especially, she said, reports that reinforced male preconceptions about "feminism." Studs Terkel's interviews in *Race* (1992) offered views from a cross-section of Americans—preachers, factory workers, gang members, interracial couples—about our "national obsession."

Terkel knows the value of engaging people in conversation, but his experiences demonstrate the risks involved in trying to distill the words of others into a comprehensible, concise account. Charlise Lyles (Cunningham, 1993), a newspaper editor Terkel profiled in *Race*, later accused Terkel of misrepresenting her views, particularly about race relations. "Where were all the positive things I had said . . . ?" Lyles said a friend told her: "This isn't the Charlise I know. You sound like one of those black folks crying victim" (p. 8). Communicating across cultures increases the odds of misunderstanding. Terkel, no doubt, believed in his portrayal of Lyles, but the episode reminds us that writer and subject do not always share a vision and ideally should explore potential differences prior to publication or broadcast.

Celebrating Heritage

Today we tend to preserve cultural roots rather than allow them to disappear in the melting pot. Preserving and celebrating cultural heritage gives people an identity, and for some, an identity reestablishes self-respect and dignity. Indeed, for some segments of the population, assertion of cultural or ethnic differences springs from a sense of disadvantage, deprivation and subjugation in relation to the rest of the society or community. Cultural heritage fuels ethnic or race pride. News organizations increasingly have recognized the importance of cultural heritage through sections or features on women, African-Americans and ethnic groups. But calendar-driven stories to mark special occasions, such as Yom Kippur or Chinese New Year's, are not as inclusive, meaningful, and satisfying as coverage that regularly writes the chapters of heritage. A conversational journalism focuses on people and events that define and validate a group's identity—as well as its inner diversity; such stories also educate a larger population that knows about middle-class traditions and little else. Cultural heritage includes a history of accomplishments, milestones, triumphs and, perhaps most important of all, outrages, such as the East St. Louis race riots of 1917, the internment of Japanese Americans in World War II, and the massacre at Wounded Knee. Persecuted minorities want to keep memories alive for themselves and their children, of course, but also for the rest of society and its children.

Seeking Diversity of Issues, Events, and Views

Diversity requires a diversity of news "sources." However, despite journalism's avowed goal of greater diversity, news reports continue to quote white males as experts on most subjects, especially foreign affairs and the economy. The experts tend to come from the same monocultural backgrounds—they are professors at elite universities, officials from government agencies, or researchers at think tanks, and they are adept at dispensing prepackaged sound bites and ready-to-print quotes. With effort, journalists might find a black, female economist to provide context for the latest Commerce Department report or a Latino teacher who specializes in Far Eastern politics. New, bi-, and multicultural perspectives from experts outside the mainstream offer possibilities of stories far more engaging than the predictable "reaction" piece. Benefits abound when journalists seek a diversity of insights; they gain exposure to new theories and views on problems provided by thoughtful people with something original to say. Reporting is a process of discovery that should value surprise over predictability. There will be few surprises for journalists who walk the same paths daily and cultivate the same fields.

Some newspapers and television news programs have brought people of color and women into the dialogue, but this does not necessarily mean they have brought in the experiences of the poor and powerless. A diversity in number is not necessarily a diversity in content. People of color and women brought in by news organizations may or may not be underprivileged or come from such backgrounds. They may or may not have conformed to a white male culture. The question is, has the content and substance of the news changed to reflect the diversity of cultures?

The young, white, suburban or urban "chic" homogeneity of journalists results in a predictable range of values and attitudes in the newsroom (Weaver, 1991). To provide balance and perspective, reporters and editors need to sample other ideologies, lifestyles, places, and activities. Journalists—all of us—can reduce our vulnerability to stereotypes by determinedly seeking multicultural experiences. These need not be in-depth projects, such as assigning a reporter to spend a month in a public housing to produce a series of articles. Journalists might simply try more often to ride the bus to work instead of driving the freeway; sit in on morning gatherings of older citizens at McDonald's; attend Friday night football games at a city high school; talk to people living at a homeless shelter; or visit a hospice for AIDS patients. Although stories might emerge from such experiences, the main object is to infuse fresh attitudes that do not simply bolster previous expectations and conventional wisdom.

Sometimes, despite good intentions and affirmative steps toward multicultural understanding, we have to admit we need help. Diversity in the newsroom—through a staff that is representative of the community—helps guard against serious lapses caused by blind spots. Mistakes occur less often in a diverse newsroom that scrutinizes stories, photos, illustrations, and images for offensive stereotypes. But the newsroom environment must also encourage diversity in viewpoints, especially when white males dominate decision-making roles. Through formal and informal means—from story conferences to open-door policies—there should be opportunities and rewards for routine participation in news decisions throughout the organization.

Bringing non-journalists into the process enhances perspectives and reduces the odds for error or bad judgment. Several news organizations have asked ordinary citizens to write columns or collaborate with staff members on news stories. NBC, for example, provided a former gang leader named Apollo with a camcorder and asked him to show outsiders life inside South Central Los Angeles. Entering some subcultures requires guides and translators who are not readily found working in newsrooms.

No story or publication can or should try to encompass all perspectives or "cultures." Nor are cultures monolithic; there are too many differences, even leading to subcultures within subcultures. News is a continuing conversation, with each story or column or broadcast a contribution to that conversation. Journalists who recognize there is no universal "black view" or "gay perspective" or "middle-class attitude" are less apt to generalize or be seen as culturally inept, for to ask someone from a minority group to serve as a spokesperson indicates a willingness to generalize about "others."

Multicultural journalism, when taken to extremes, inhibits rather than enhances dialogue and perspective building. Guilt-driven multicultural efforts by journalists determined to make amends for past omissions can lead to bland, Chamber of Commerce–type stories about a "heroic" inner city teacher, an "inspiring" single mother who put seven children through college, or a "courageous" paraplegic who climbs mountains "despite" the disability. Indeed, some stories might be killed or toned down for fear of offending minorities or ethnics. People who have been coping within the dominant culture all their lives do not appreciate condescending, patronizing, or paternalistic coverage. Nor do they appreciate having a single person anointed to symbolize the multiplicity of concerns represented by a race, a gender, an ethnic group, or a life-style.

MULTIDISCIPLINARY RESPONSIBILITIES FOR A "FLOATING JOURNALISM"

Complementing a multicultural perspective must be a multidisciplinary approach to journalism. Without multidisciplinary interests, journalism, with its natural and headline-induced tendency to rely on impressionistic "data," risks misinterpreting people and situations. Journalism, as a discipline, benefits from the rigorous research methodologies employed by historians, psychologists, sociologists, and other behavioral scientists. Much of what journalists produce is intended to be fragmentary, anecdotal, and freestanding—reports about arrests, fires, groundbreakings, bank closings, jail breaks. While such news has its place, it is a *floating journalism* minus context. The methods of other disciplines help journalists to see events, people, and nature more broadly and realistically.

No news report represents a complete, indisputable account of an event or condition. If news is, as James Carey (1986) said, a curriculum, then journalists should be as diligent as archaeologists, sifting for cultural artifacts, or as watchful as sociologists and anthropologists, observing patterns of behavior and customs. Other disciplines, particularly history, provide a diversity of views within an explanatory context. Other disciplines recognize the dangers of relying on too few sources, looking for people to blame or searching for an ultimate answer when none may exist.

Stories with facts and opinions in isolation from a larger view lack importance and appeal; such stenographic reportage rarely engages people. In fact, the typical straight news story that attempts to explain a problem actually discourages conversation. It usually is based on quotes from experts and it carries an implicit message: "Here's the situation; here's what you need to know; there's little else to say." Even detailed stories—so-called in-depth pieces— often fail to fuel conversation. They may provide expert sources but nevertheless tend to suggest, in the end that no one agrees on the problem or issue at hand. The reader reacts, "What the hell. If experts can't sort it out, how can I? Why should I even bother?" News ought to invite more talk, not serve up take-it-or leave-it answers.

Journalism typically aims for a sense of closure by producing self-contained, free-standing news accounts. Leaving loose ends suggests an incomplete assignment. In school and newsroom, young reporters hear: "Your job isn't to raise social questions, it's to answer them." While questions are necessary, it is dangerous to believe that answers must be immediate. Often they emerge slowly and laboriously over time. In some instances, raising questions and leaving them hanging helps in the search for answers. Open-ended accounts invite further discussion, bringing more opinions into the marketplace; they invite creative thinking, like presenting children with a Rubik's cube puzzle or tricky riddle. "How does it do that?" "Why is that happening?" The best stories challenge and intrigue; they encourage and map further exploration tomorrow, next week, or next month.

A multidisciplinary sensitivity in journalism would also focus on the human condition within larger cultural and ecological contexts. The Native American holistic and ecological philosophies suggest one type of diversity needed in newsrooms. Geneticist David Suzuki (Suzuki & Knudtson, 1992) appreciated the orientation of Native Americans and other indigenous people. As the chief of the Nuu Cha Nulth people in Canada once told Suzuki, "If the water can no longer support the salmon, if the land can't support deer and bear, then why do we think it will support us?" Suzuki observed: "From this attitude of respect, gratitude, and humility, aboriginal people have acquired an understanding of their 'relatives' that is far more extensive than the uni-dimensional kind of information that is gleaned by scientists" (p. xxxv). Journalists, too, define news by human and often political priorities, often failing to include the interconnections of people to wildlife, plants, soil, and water.

News both reflects and defines our culture. In producing their narratives, journalists influence who we are as individuals and as a society. In sociology, for example, reportage of news events has been studied as "constructed" reality, with journalism determining how we interpret a set of circumstances or occurrences. Journalists do not just report stories but "frame" them, deciding the shape, tone, content, depth, breadth, and focus of the news. The story in narrative form helps people understand their places in what is going on. A story offers a beginning, middle, and end; it identifies principal characters, describes their actions, and explains, when possible, their motives. Narrative news stories provide a context for our collective public life; they provide meaning by providing a context in which isolated events may be integrated. Historian William Cronon (1992) observed that narrative history can be viewed as "an endless struggle among competing narratives and values" (p. 1370), which could be said of news narratives as well. Journalists, like historians, must make choices about which stories to tell and how to tell them. The choices ultimately depend on the range of perspectives available.

Ecumenical and multiperspectival reporting reconsider traditional ways of defining news and therefore the means of obtaining it. Breaking news must be noted immediately, but its importance should be weighed with other more enduring, substantive news in mind. A terrorist bomb that kills six children at a department store merits reportage; from another perspective, the daily terrorism of central city living looms larger. Beat-generated news, too, remains important, but reallocating the time reporters spend on "big government" and "big business" to schools, homes, small businesses, and the streets offers fresher perspective. News in a broader, ecumenical definition includes relationships among people, their conditions, and their environments. News, in this sense, examines not only suffering, destruction, despair, and disintegration, but also hope, inspiration, guidance, direction, and common ground.

By making social groups more accessible to each other, journalists do more than acknowledge the values of others and their viewponts; such receptivity—expressed in both philosophy and practice—exposes journalists to a diversity of critical reviews by which to judge the accuracy, fairness and diligence of their own roles. Journalists write and report as members of a community but invariably shade the dialogue with their own biases. Journalists need a check, as do historians or others who interpret and assess society—a self-correcting, homeostatic social mechanism. A finely crafted story about the crime-infested neighborhood may be "true" from the reporter's vantage point, but the people of the neighborhood may claim that the reporter saw and heard little of what they experience. An ecumenical orientation may not prevent myopic reporting, but it clearly contributes more directly and forcefully to a dialogic public that feels rhetorically included, represented, and able to make a difference.

5

Connecting with the Community: Journalism and Responsibility

Weekly editors, with their windows on Main Street, seem comfortably and naturally connected to their communities, understanding with clarity their roles and responsibilities. "Towns need to be stimulated and inspired," said one editor (Kennedy, 1974). "They require the catalytic action of a newspaper that keeps suggesting ways to make the town's life better" (p. 246). "I have hoped to make my newspaper a community necessity. I have wanted to provide an institution whose demise would leave an irreplaceable hole. I haven't wanted people to take my paper or leave it" (p. 244).

In some ways, the weekly editor represents the ideal of community-oriented journalism. For the aggressively independent small-town newspaper, which lives in memories or memoirs, if rarely in small towns, bonds the editor with the community in print once a week and face-to-face—at the grocery store, church supper, and street corner—as a daily relationship. The model weekly editor both collects and conveys the community's news and opinions in a personal, intimate way. Together, newspaper and editor stimulate and monitor the community's conversation, and from that conversation emerges the community's clarified aspirations and values.

It is an ideal some journalists find romantic, sentimental, and delusional, but it appeals to journalists who desire an enhanced sense of purpose.

In an age of diminished expectations for public discourse, coupled with distrust of media messengers, news organizations struggle to rediscover the seemingly lost links to people and communities. Self-interest motivates part of the effort toward "connecting" with community life, for a thriving, peaceful community means residual prosperity for the business of news. However, beyond economic concerns lies another motivation, inspired by a mission to reestablish, as well, a central role in a democratic, multicultural society. Journalism seeks—perhaps the phrase "longs for" is more apt—a vitality and significance of purpose to renew its own self-worth. The roles of entertainer and marketer of news fail to satisfy that longing.

Society, too, seeks its own natural condition—a common ground where people live together and function with a sense of control over their destinies. Ross Perot captured the imagination and votes of millions of Americans, promising change and empowerment. His message resonated: "Something's wrong, something needs to be done, and you can do it—seize the moment." While Perot did not speak convincingly to a multicultural constituency, he did elicit a response that journalism must envy. He and other candidates had an impact by talking with ordinary citizens. Journalism need not mobilize a community or solve its problems to rediscover vitality. It is enough to connect people increasingly divided by physical, economic, political, and emotional suspicions and to help the community search for a shared vision that might lead to the resolution of common problems.

We begin by defining the concept of community, asking: What is this "community" news organizations court? How is it defined and what are its qualities? What role should news organizations play in the community—building, persuading, energizing, or merely reporting? The answers that emerge will not satisfy every journalist or news organization, but by exploring the questions, we develop a fuller understanding of journalism's potential.

A COMMUNITY VIEW

Robert Nisbet (1990) said that we are driven by a "quest of community." This was the theme of his influential book by the same name, which was first published in 1953 and was reissued in 1970 and again in 1990. Nisbet's enduring work—which may be even more relevant today than forty years ago—asks us to explore new forms of community rather than to revive a nostalgic community of yesterday. The comfortable and appealing qualities of small-town America simply do not reflect much of contemporary life. In fact, millions of people have been forced from farms and small towns. Urban development projects uprooted people, forcing them out of relatively cohesive neighborhoods into public housing. Job transfers have kept white-collar families in flux, relocating from one suburban enclave to another. Immigrants have congregated in cities and towns (and not only in urban Miami, Los Angeles and New York), holding tight to their cultural and social belongings. African-Americans and other minority groups have increasingly resisted full-scale assimilation into the mainstream. Gays and lesbians, once closeted by choice or by treatment, now have asserted an identity. More than ever before, the United States is a nation of multiple communities, some based on geography, and many based on associations. Nisbet argued that the diversity, autonomy, and vigor of our communities and associations protect us from the dangers of a centralized, politically powerful national community with its imposed conformity. He encouraged community on a human scale through fraternal lodges, farm bureaus, church groups, and block clubs. Pluralism defines us and our communities, which is generally for the good.

But within a pluralistic society, pockets of smaller communities, both territorial and associational, struggle to retain identity and solidarity within a larger community of competing values, priorities and goals. As a result, contemporary community—particularly in the city—experiences frequent conflicts and crises, which we sometimes loosely call "breakdowns" of community. As subcommunities express themselves, airing grievances and seeking rights and entitlements within the larger community, further splintering occurs—resulting in smaller groups that are communities unto themselves. At the extreme are separatist communities such as some survivalist groups and religious cults like the Branch Davidians, in Waco, Texas, whose physical and ideological borders were closed to outsiders who would not commit totally.

Community building and maintenance pose challenges, but community does not depend on cohesion or absence of conflict. Dangers arise primarily when access to communication is precluded or presumed impossible. Hostage negotiators in a standoff "keep the lines of communication open"; suicide prevention counselors follow the rule, "Keep them talking." For communities in turmoil and at risk, the advice fits especially well. When talk succeeds, it often heads off the need to communicate with bottles and bullets. If communication cannot guarantee harmony, it can at least enable harmony. The ultimate community, some say, is a community based on inquiry. Glenn Tinder (1980) argued that community can only exist if people "insist again and again, by speech and occasionally by violent resistance, that not any kind of unity that habit, circumstances, or a momentary elite can induce everyone to accept is a community" (p. 31). Through inquiry, Tinder said, people together test and sometimes enhance the value of what they share.

The essence of community remains people connected by a shared experience and fate. As John Dewey (1916) wrote more than seventy-five years ago, "There is more than a verbal tie between the words common, community and communication. Men live in a community in virtue of the things which they have in common; and communication is the way in which they come to possess things in common" (p. 5). To Nisbet (1990), community "is founded on man, conceived in his wholeness, rather than in one or another of the roles, taken separately, that he may hold in a social order. Community is a fusion of feeling and thought, of tradition and commitment, of membership and volition" (pp. 47, 48). While a brand of individualism marks our national character, a sense of belonging remains a powerful force, especially when disintegration, rootlessness, alienation, and conflict leave people feeling unsettled or insecure. Most people seek communal life. Community, though, means more than "belonging to." It is a "belonging with." Community creates another level of life—a common, symbiotic existence. "Community," in one respect, functions as society's velcro, connecting smaller clusters of individuals and their interests, forming public entities—*a community* (a city or region) *of communities* (clusters of affiliation within a city or region).

The aggregate community, then, exists when its people can talk to produce—if possible—meaning, understanding, and direction. News organizations, especially local newspapers, should occupy a prominent place in a community's life and conversation. Viewing community as a place of inquiry asks journalists to consider what messages and dialogue are necessary to increase the perception of commonalities among, for example, Hispanics and Asian-Americans, Jews and African-Americans, suburbanites and inner-city residents. A community exists when people hold different views and values but still feel connected. Journalism can help people discuss both differences and similarities.

With inquiry and conversation as its complementary themes, journalism can encourage a definition of community that transcends political boundaries or local associations to include people of other cities, regions, states, and nations. Defining community narrowly by audience surveys, circulation zones, or signal strength, as news organizations sometimes do, unnecessarily limits opportunities. A broader, more expansive definition better reflects a pluralistic yet interdependent society.

JOURNALISM'S RELATIONSHIP TO COMMUNITY

The relationship of journalism to community remains influenced by the lasting ideas of Robert Park and John Dewey, who viewed communication as the key to public life. Park (1955) cited the newspaper's role in maintaining a Jeffersonian democracy. "The newspaper must continue to tell us about ourselves," he said. "We must somehow learn to know our community and its affairs in the same intimate way in which we know them in the country villages" (p. 93). For Dewey, community depended on face-to-face communication. Personalized, evocative, socially relevant news, Dewey believed, could approximate interpersonal communication and further stimulate the conversation that fuels community life.

Putting the Dewey-Park principles into practice requires that news organizations aspire to communication more than information. The difference is crucial. Information is a commodity; communication is a mutual process of developing shared meaning. If we believe that producing information is synonymous with communicating, we will continue to blame audiences for shortcomings of context and inadequacies of vision. To communicate means far more attention by news organizations to listening and learning.

Reconstituting journalism as conversation presents problems because news organizations are not accustomed to communicating. News, in its most prevalent form, has been commodified (a point reinforced in Chapter 3). Facts and information are gathered, then delivered to the doorsteps or living rooms of consumers. When news constitutes a commodity, the relationship of news organization to the community remains one of power and authority of the *sender* over the *receiver*, the teller's dominion over the told. News rolls off the assembly line daily, and the consumer is expected to sign off on the delivery generally without question. After all, the news is the news. From a consumerist perspective, discourse about the news may be interesting but ultimately is largely futile.

News, in a more fundamental sense, emerges as a community converses with itself. News defines us and we, in turn, define the news in a never-ending process, which is why more members of the community must be included in the process. News as it *could be*—a cocreation of journalists and community members—stimulates further communication among coworkers, families, teachers, and politicians, which ultimately leads back to journalists. To join the conversation as a catalyst and collaborator, journalism must reposition news, seeing it as more than collectable facts and documentable information. News is a collaborative activity of people negotiating their different interpretations into newly shaped, shared meanings. News, in other words, is the communication of social change.

For too long, journalists have considered the news a public concern but its definition a private domain; outsiders—unskilled, uninitiated and naive—would likely botch or contaminate the process of news "making." That mentality, though now under scrutiny, nonetheless persists, reinforcing the perception of news as commodity. In its format and delivery, news is transmitted to the community but rarely communicated. News of government, for example, focuses on legislation—debate, compromises, political intrigue, voting. The community, forced into a spectator's role, is *told* about legislation but rarely expected to discuss it let alone determine its content. The community, however, appears eager for involvement, as the 1992 presidential elections demonstrated. During the campaign, several news organizations, including the *Charlotte Observer*, moved closer to a communication model by inviting voters to question the candidates directly. For their part, some candidates, preempting the traditional press role, offered voters opportunities for direct talk at public forums and on TV, cable, and radio call-in programs. People eagerly joined in, and they sometimes asked smart, tough questions, causing some to wonder if the political reporters were superfluous. If the news in part defines us and our communities, then it is too important to be left solely in the hands of journalists. Moreover, news cannot find its natural condition until the community—through its many components—can ask questions and express itself in its procreative role. The public and the press need each other in a partnership of civic, political activity.

This partnership is not just an economic marriage of convenience. A journalistic emphasis on community and public life develops citizens, not consumers. Nearly everyone holds some notion of citizenship—whether voter, law-abiding member of the community, political activist, or political outcast. Citizenship can be felt in terms of national pride; it can be experienced by petitioning the city council; it can be threatened by a violation of rights; it can be meaningless to those on the fringes of society. For all but the most destitute and helpless, people stand ready to reclaim some semblance of citizenship if only they could feel enabled to do so. Communicating with a community of citizens does not require that news organizations abandon what they do now; the community still depends on consumer-oriented news about bank mergers, road repairs, convenience store holdups, medical breakthroughs, and stock-market conditions; people rely on journalists to maintain a vigilant watch over important matters that they cannot monitor. The primary change involves a new purpose and direction for the news—community-focused, representative, and helpful as a means for people to find, individually and collectively, fulfillment, security, and well-being in their lives. A sense of self, community and, ultimately, citizenship comes from involvement and doing things, not being told, "You're OK" or "You are somebody"—or worse, "The news is so complicated and confusing nowadays. We'll tell you what to think and when to worry." When people feel respected and effective as participants in community life, they are more likely to converse and act as citizens. News organizations can help them achieve conversation and find meaning in citizenship.

News organizations that offer news as contributions to conversation accept a responsibility to open and maintain lines of communication *actively* within a diverse, and often fragmented, community. The responsibility extends to identifying problems, establishing agreed-upon values, developing priorities for action, arriving at goals and objectives for governing and living and helping the community realize its ambitions. It is easier to practice what journalism used to refer to as "Afghanistanism"—writing daringly and expressing ire about distant places and problems. To engage in community-building requires an ethical commitment, something news outlets—with newspapers at the forefront—demand of others but not always of themselves, as they report and editorialize about banking institutions that redline neighborhoods and deny people loans, of hospitals that turn away indigent patients or dump them at public hospitals, of businesses, like General Motors, and how they exploit and then abandon communities, such as Flint, Michigan. What of news organizations? Are they redlining, turning away, exploiting, and abandoning? What relationship do the outlets for news have with their communities? Does self-interest at times come first—winning awards, garnering acclaim from peers, selling more papers, or luring a large audience? Is it enough to report the news, good and bad, in a truthful, accurate way and assume that the people will be served? In the communication model, a news organization's responsibility does not begin and end with publication or broadcast of an ethically sound *product*.

If journalism recreates the town commons, then it provides the space for conversation, entering into the talk as well. But it does not necessarily provide answers. Journalism contributes as an integral part of a process through which questions surface for debate that, it is hoped, will lead to illumination or clarification. News organizations undermine the process when they limit it to exchanges between journalists and their expert sources, whose opinions often misrepresent the reality of people entangled in issues. News organizations that open the floor for diverse, intense discourse acknowledge a partnership in communication and demonstrate confidence that a responsive citizenry can produce solutions to societal problems.

Within a pluralistic community, establishing lines of communication, especially where none previously existed, requires time and patient nurturing. Stages of communication-building might be necessary—a stepladder approach. The bottom rung is community tolerance, perhaps the lowest common denominator. Here people reach a level of coexistence. Next comes acceptance, through which the community reflects a willingness to welcome others as neighbors, coworkers, and even friends. Then comes collaboration—community members working together on common concerns. At the topmost rung is consensus, when the community goes beyond coexistence, neighborliness, and collaboration to achieve agreement on a course of action or behavior. Not every community, certainly not on every issue, will develop consensus. It is enough to know that a community possesses the means by which to agree and act toward identified ends. Habermas (1992), for example, has identified an "ideal speech situation" as one in which all participants not only have equal access to significant speaking and listening situations but also are not systematically excluded from the decision making that ensues from such situations. The consensus that could—but may not necessarily—develop is one that an enlightened journalism could enable. (See Habermas, 1992, pp. 92–93, 125, 170, for more recent thinking on this topic.) Of course, as some theorists have stressed, it is the ability of different groups to be heard and to influence the action in society that is primarily important, not the achievement of consensus (Young, 1990).

Local news organizations must demand that people in communities do more than consume news; they must motivate listening, stimulate thinking, and provide opportunities for citizens to sound off. Provocative stories, of course, invite participation, stirring people to talk and action. Public opinion polls, letters to the editor, readers' advocates, and the like remain important and potentially well-used methods of communication. However, the conversation begun through the news needs to continue after publication and broadcast in interpersonal, interactive formats. Some news organizations are aiding just that type of interaction, sponsoring public forums, ascertaining community needs, providing computer bulletin boards and 1-800 lines, bringing people into editorial meetings, and hiring neighborhood writers. When news organizations make a commitment to get people talking, help them connect with one another, and then listen responsively to what is being said, participation follows. As William Greider (1992) argues in *Who Will Tell the People?*, news organizations determined to bring people back into public life "create a space for them in the political debate and draw them into it" (p. 304). A responsible news organization, he said, "would learn how to teach and listen and agitate. It would invent new formats that provide a tangible context in which people can understand power and also speak to it" (p. 304). If initial efforts result in a marginal response from the community, the communication lines should stay in place, for thousands still profit from eavesdropping, as do listeners to talk radio programs. Eventually, even eavesdroppers enter and extend the conversation.

Bill Moyers (1992) is one voice in a growing chorus celebrating the reemergence of the American citizen who seeks a democratic voice in determining his or her way of life. Moyers pointed to the *Philadelphia Inquirer*'s impressive series on the nation's economy, "America: What Went Wrong." "It was about tax policy, health care, pension rules, corporate debt and the bankruptcy code—all that 'stuff' we usually think no one wants to read about," said Moyers (p. 5D). But people overran the newspaper's lobby for reprints, with more than 400,000 eventually being distributed. (The series was later published in book form, further demonstrating the public interest.) In Moyers's words, "[People] will respond to a press that stimulates the community without pandering to it, that inspires people to embrace their responsibilities without lecturing or hectoring them, that engages their better natures without sugarcoating ugly realities or patronizing their foibles" (p. 5D). It appears that a receptive citizenry awaits a news media that recognizes its responsibilities to democracy. It rewards a media system that recognizes that democracy is, at its base, a mode of talking more than a mode of governing. Democracy is not what a government does, but instead, how a public ratifies, through conversation, having a government in the first place.

To this point, our ideas represent a philosophical approach to conversational journalism. To apply that philosophy—to talk to people of the community and give them the means to talk to journalists and to each other—leads to practical considerations. How does journalism connect with the community? What do news organizations report, and in which formats? How does journalism assist in community building and citizenship?

KNOWING AND BUILDING THE COMMUNITY

Writer Jane Jacobs (1961), a champion of city life, told of visiting the North End of Boston in 1959 and experiencing the rebirth of the neighborhood's sense of community—seeing children playing and people shopping, strolling, and talking. "The general street atmosphere of buoyancy, friendliness and good health was so infectious that I began asking directions of people just for the fun of getting in on some talk," Jacobs wrote in her classic book, *The Death and Life of Great American Cities*, over thirty years ago. Today's journalists can discover and appreciate city life from her observations and ideas. As they look and listen for stories about their own communities, they might imitate Jacobs by walking down streets, through neighborhoods, asking questions, seeking directions, and talking to people about where they live, work, and play. They will hear different things, but they will not improve on her method.

Journalists who are too comfortable within the confines of the newsroom or city hall drive to and from work oblivious to their surroundings and stick to routines of working, shopping, or socializing. Many might lack a prerequisite for informed, sensitive and lively community coverage—curiosity. From curiosity springs another perspective—receptivity. A community, above all else, is a collage of people who differ in ideology, vision, experience, and concerns. No one individual—no spokesperson—can speak for a community. It is the journalist's challenge and opportunity to sample a community's diversity with an open mind, a keen eye and a sensitive ear. Charles Kuralt (1985) offered one appealing model of journalism that is sensitive to people and places through his series "On the Road." In Kuralt's words, "I have tried to go slow, stick to the back roads, take time to meet people, listen to yarns, notice the countryside go by, and feel the seasons change" (p. 14). *Meet. Listen. Notice. Feel*: that is a good motto for journalism.

Going into the community, however, will not guarantee understanding. Journalists presume to tell people what is happening in the community—what is wrong and who is to blame. Yet the people about whom journalists report often find news accounts grossly incomplete or distorted. Good intentions alone cannot compensate for a journalist's impaired vision or hearing. An empathic eye and ear help, but a diversity of approaches, including ones that enlist nonjournalists in telling stories, can ensure more representative accounts of the community.

Journalism professor Jay Rosen (1991b) recently noted the different ways in which the *New York Times* and *Newsday* covered New York City's subway system. *Newsday* assigned a reporter to write a column, "In the Subways," based on the reporter's experiences as a daily subway rider and observer, while the *Times* covered the system primarily from the perspective of the transit authority. "*Newsday*'s approach," Rosen said, "starts with common life." He observed that the transit authority "is not a location where the newspaper can connect itself to the common life of the city" (p. 18). The comparison of *Newsday* versus the *Times* asks us to consider where we look for news—within bureaucracies or on the streets. Of course, both must be monitored, but committed journalists cannot shrink from the job of community reporting—they must venture forth. In some cases, no bureaucracy represents or regulates certain groups. Homeless people who sleep on park benches belong to the community and the community belongs to them. If journalists fail to tell the diverse stories of a community, who will?

In more specific terms, how do journalists discover a community's "relevance"? How do they experience the city and interact with its people? The answer is obvious: by meeting people and experiencing their lives.

- Converse with at least one "real" person a day—a cabbie, street vendor, retiree—not necessarily in search of a story, but rather in search of new perspectives and contexts for stories, as some news organizations do in inventive ways.
- Quote public officials when necessary, but for every public official, talk to three "ordinary" people from the com-

munity—not necessarily to quote them, but to understand more thoroughly how their discourse might respond to that of the officials, and how it might potentially change the official viewpoint.

- Collaborate with community people through "my story" assignments, in which a barber, let's say, tells his own story in his own words. It might be about a holdup he witnessed or even something less dramatic, like how he became a barber. The reporter's job would be to make the story readable, relevant, and accessible.

- Expand the Rolodex to include nontraditional sources— people like a social worker, the volunteer director of a food bank, a minister of a storefront church—who can help journalists understand, interpret, and critique what community officials are saying and doing about crime, taxes, welfare programs, and other areas where policy is being made, laws passed, and public money spent.

- Seek cross-cultural, cross-generational experiences, as by inviting an international student to lunch or home for dinner or volunteering to help out at a Veterans Hospital or nursing home. If a story emerges, fine; if not, the personal benefit for the journalist comes from expanded context for the news.

- Attend—and attend to—community-building events such as neighborhood fairs and church suppers. The time and effort required will be repaid with a heightened sensitivity to future stories.

- Sponsor "news dialogue" meetings in the community, during which reporters, photographers, editors, and news directors (1) directly hear public responses to past stories; (2) probe community sentiments for revised news policies; and (3) encourage citizens to address each other's hopes and fears for the community.

While it is impossible to connect with all who reside in a community, it is possible to reasonably *characterize* and even *represent* the community, with special emphasis on those people with fewer opportunities to engage in the community's conversation, such as nursing home residents, the mentally challenged, and the array of people who have lost control over their lives. Going to unfamiliar places leads the journalist to a community of interests, fears and aspirations that are invisible from the freeway or office tower.

Beyond meeting people, listening, and learning from them, journalists help to build a community by disclosing the diversity and rich experiences of its people and places, relating stories about neighborhood spirit, ethnic traditions, and racial heritage as discussed more fully in Chapter 4. The stories include those about people who find belonging critical to their lives—computer clubs, religious sects, and extended families, for example. From individual stories emerges a fuller identity and sense of community. While some stories of community life produce disturbing, disquieting pictures, telling them is necessary for people to know and appreciate one another. The community, so revealed, becomes more familiar and less foreboding.

Looking back builds community, as well. History provides a frame for a community's present condition and suggests its future. It is a touchstone for journalists who are serious about discovering a community and telling its stories. In cities certainly, but also in many smaller towns (especially suburban ones), newcomers want a more personal connection with where they live. They know little beyond the fact, for example, that the railroad tracks used to divide blacks from whites or that the neighborhood grade school bears a woman's name, that of the first woman in the region to be so honored. News organizations can unearth the community's roots, teaching how the city developed its particularly intense pride in its schools or the extent of civic cooperation when a tornado leveled the courthouse in 1955. A diverse history is needed, not a narrow textbook version that paints the past in a coat of innocence. Relating the ugly side of the community's history, while unpleasant, must also become a part of communal introspection. People curious about a community's past will be better prepared to contribute to its future. Journalists maintain and contribute to the community's history—its collective memory and reference points; newspapers, especially, operate as the institutional memory of an area. That role can be expanded to less formal human institutions, such as families, and more human-scale memories as well, told word-of-mouth. Accounts of a community's history should be connected to the present. In that way, history becomes not simply a relic, but a living, breathing, and vital part of the community.

Exploring the community yields its rewards, but after venturing forth, meeting people, experiencing other life-styles, visiting neighborhoods, and reflecting on history, can we then define our community? Can we arrive at an inventory of human, natural, and emotional components, cross currents, and characteristics that not only define the community but explain it as well? Even in its diversity, a community can have a discernible character, just as a person with different moods and experiences can be said to have a personality. Community news rarely delves into the identity of a town or city. Rarely does news examine a community's psyche— its spiritual, emotional, and moral side. Once we know the human and physical elements of a community, can we say the job is complete without at least attempting to discover the community's character? Entering this unfamiliar realm of news puts journalists into roles of criticism and diagnosis. Journalists are not psychoanalysts, and to presume special therapeutic skill is dangerous. However, with care, and outside expertise if necessary, journalism can explore the inner community, looking particularly for pathologies long denied and subtle social and linguistic clues that could lead to healthier cooperation among groups.

A penetrating diagnosis of the community will sweep journalism into the churning waters of values reporting, testing a news organization's commitment to community. Values reporting means elucidating and questioning the fundamental beliefs, attitudes, and behavior of the community and its people. If news organizations assume a role in building community, it follows that the news should concentrate on the bricks and mortar of the community life—family, neighborhood, church, schools and other primary associations—and the soul of the community—honesty, tolerance, shared responsibility, hospitality and charity.

CONNECTING WITH COMMUNITY: JOURNALISM AS THERMOSTAT

Understanding the community and sharing that understanding builds community peripherally. The crucial step for news organizations—connecting with community—presents complications associated with boosterism and conflicts of interest. Knowing where to draw the line becomes difficult, particularly for news organizations conditioned to remain apart from the community for fear of losing objectivity or balance. Fairness and balance stand as worthy ideals, but news organizations cannot timidly address the community and help its people without leadership in the community's life. A return to crusading, public-spirited journalism might be in order.

A philosophy of community-based journalism can be found in the experience of Richard H. Amberg, the publisher of the *St. Louis Globe-Democrat* from 1955 to his death in 1967 (Killenberg, 1968). Amberg took over a 103-year-old newspaper that was fading in 1955 into economic and professional oblivion. He transformed the *Globe-Democrat*, enabling it to compete seriously with its formidable—and richer—rival, the *St. Louis Post-Dispatch*. Under Amberg, "Fighting FOR St. Louis" became the newspaper's slogan, which he emblazoned on its delivery trucks. Amberg joined or created dozens of local organizations, heading, for example, a multimillion-dollar fund-raising construction drive for a new local hospital. His crusades extended from the editorial page into the news, one of them an unrelenting campaign for a free bridge to link St. Louis to its adjacent cities and towns in Illinois.

Amberg once said most newspapers were either thermostats or thermometers. His newspaper was a thermostat, he said, for it told more than the temperature—it took effective action. "The editorial page and its extension into other parts of the paper, in the form of editorial crusades, is the heart and soul and mind of a newspaper," he said (Killenberg, 1968, p. 109). "A newspaper should be the leader in community thinking and action, and it should translate news and opinions into forcible action whenever and wherever it can, by whatever means are at its disposal" (p. 109). Amberg's counterpart, Joseph Pulitzer, told a *Time* reporter, "[Amberg] gets into every nook and cranny. I try to be careful to disassociate myself from boards and committees that could distort my news judgment." Amberg countered: "I believe that a man running a newspaper cannot properly know what goes on in his community unless he is a part of it" (p. 116). In effect, Amberg's thermostatic comparison announced journalism's optimal function in the communication system of community. Journalism is the feedback mechanism through which we can (1) sense the social temperature, (2) compare it to previous plans and decisions, and (3) recalibrate the system to provide a closer social match between what we have and what we need. Feedback systems do not just observe; they monitor and react. Beyond reporting conditions accurately, they mobilize the system for change.

Richard Amberg exhibited, at times, a self-righteous zeal for projects and crusades. While willing to walk arm and arm with people on projects he endorsed, if opposed, he would not hesitate to grab the community by the scruff of the neck. And though deeply involved in community affairs, Amberg and his newspaper often stiffly *told* people what to think and do, as opposed to following the collaborative path of community dialogue. Nevertheless, even though he was not always an exemplar of our conversational journalism, Amberg stimulated and led the community to action. His newspapers empowered citizens, long before that concept became fashionable, by encouraging the organization of neighborhood groups, inciting people to call and lobby public officials and appealing for community support of civic and charitable projects. An example shows his technique and its results. In 1956, he decided the city needed a then-rare $65,000 heart-lung pump for use in pediatric heart operations; only three were in use at the time—two at the Mayo Clinic and one at a Philadelphia medical school. With a front-page editorial for donations, he asked: "What is it worth to you to save the lives of 300 children a year?" The newspaper printed the names of each donor, and within two weeks, more than $100,000 had been raised. Amberg wrote a thank-you note to each contributor, even those who were able to afford only a few dollars (Killenberg, 1968, p. 33).

Increasingly, today's editors and news directors are crossing the traditional line of detachment, choosing participation in community life. An often-cited case (Rosen & Taylor, 1992) involved the *Columbus* (Georgia) *Ledger-Enquirer*, which produced a series on city issues called "Columbus Beyond 2000" and then sponsored town meetings for community discussion and action. After the town meeting, the editor of the newspaper, the late Jack Swift, held a barbecue at his home for seventy-five citizens. The gathering generated formation of a civic organization named United Beyond 2000. Swift's involvement continued when he joined with an African-American judge for a series of backyard cookouts at their homes, with each man inviting a dozen or so friends. Newcomers were added to each barbecue, and a diverse network based on friendship and common objectives emerged. The efforts results in renewed public discussion through formal and informal social networks across racial and class barriers, paving the way for a larger coalition that could address the city's future. Swift boldly entered the community's political life instead of observing it from a safe distance.

Several news organizations, such as Gannett Co., Inc., have relaxed their ethics rules regarding community participation and membership in groups so that reporters and editors can mix with more people. News organizations might consider going a step farther—encouraging staffers to seek associations, such as volunteer work, in unfamiliar parts of community where they can make new acquaintances and experience life from other vantage points. The current *St. Louis Post-Dispatch* editor, William Woo, echoed Richard Amberg's beliefs about the importance of understanding the community (1992). A week after attending the 1992 convention of the American Society of Newspaper Editors, Woo spoke at a prayer breakfast of a suburban St. Louis Kiwanis Club with a membership of forty-one. More than 300 men and women showed up for a discussion on ethics and journalism, and Woo later described the prayer breakfast to colleagues at an editorial conference: "Like most big-city papers, we do not regularly cover such events. In fact, I suspect that many journalists, like myself, have little personal experience with them. Yet here at 7 A.M. were 300 people, paying $5 a ticket, listening to a 25-minute speech without a single joke—and not a cough or a scraping chair in the audience. Here, in short, was a piece of community fabric, revealing something about the people" (p. B1).

Volunteering for community service represents a substantial investment of energy and time, but the dividends, too, are substantial. Not only does community involvement open avenues for talk, it sends a message of caring and commitment to the community. In some ways, contributing to the community through a checkbook, even when the figures add up, constitutes a smaller investment. We are not discounting the philanthropic activities of news organizations, for they do good work in the community, but checkbook charity could also be accompanied by a complementary campaign by journalists to volunteer time and talent in civic service and outreach. Community organizations, for example, typically have newsletters that need writers, content and advice that journalists could easily contribute. More visits by journalists to the public schools would be another community-building gesture by which journalism could improve its involvement and image within the community while it more effectively puts its ear on the ground.

Connecting with the community is not without risk. Journalists and news organizations could become entangled in accusations about their undue influence in public issues. We propose community involvement as long as journalists remain fair and unprejudiced. The benefits of involvement in community affairs outweigh the risks, it seems, when journalists operate with good will and the best interests of the community at heart. Citizens who see the news organization reaching out in word and deed may still disagree with the message but grow to respect the messenger.

CHANNELS OF COMMUNICATION

The obvious, conventional channels of communication remain letters to the editor or station manager and, at some newspapers, to readers' advocates. A smaller but growing number of news organizations have turned to interactive information services, such as 1-800 lines or electronic bulletin boards. The standard feedback mechanisms of news media are effective to a degree, but they only engage people with sufficient motivation or capability to respond. Moreover, people will not communicate via feedback without at least a modicum of confidence that their words and opinions matter.

For communication to reach a level of community conversation, other channels are needed, including town forums and citizen roundtables designed to voice and explore community issues and attitudes initially stimulated by news reports. In Columbus, Georgia, the newspaper-sponsored forum inspired a continuing conversation through civic groups and their activities. However, if nothing more than talk results from interpersonal gatherings, they can still be considered successful steps toward community building. News organizations appropriately organize, sponsor, and moderate community gatherings; they should also expand community conversation by encouraging forums initiated by other institutions in the community—churches, schools, hospitals, civic groups, and city government, to name a few. News organizations, however, should assume the principal responsibility for sharing the conversation from such gatherings with others in the community.

Reaching segments of the community that cannot—or will not—participate in public gatherings requires a time-consuming canvassing of the community done in places seldom visited or "covered" by reporters—nursing homes, schoolrooms, jails, and

street corners. Asking questions about "public life" is unlikely to
be effective among people who find a stranger's inquiries suspicious at best and who may wonder (and rightly so), why anyone
would care about their views. At first, it is enough to meet people,
listening and observing; questions can come later with another
visit. Communication, tenuous as it might be, has begun, and it can
be nurtured by as simple a step as leaving a business card as a
reminder and encouragement. Regular contact—once a month,
say—is communication in its own right. It conveys the message
that someone is listening, someone cares. "Journalists descend like
vultures," some citizens say, "when there's been a wreck, a crisis
or a bizarre story. Otherwise we don't see them." No doubt more
informal contact through small talk—sometimes called *phatic
communion* by social scientists—would lessen public cynicism of
the media.

Every method and mode of communication must be viewed by
journalists as an *opportunity*, not as a chore comparable to being
asked by an editor to handle a "crackpot's" call. The proper
attitude of communication extends beyond mere receptivity to
include accountability. Journalists, reinforced by the news organization's institutional commitment, must be prepared to accept
responsibility for their role in communication, recognizing that
the news does not belong to them exclusively. A willingness to
share control of the news does not come easily to some journalists, who often claim "ownership" of a story. Moreover, when
you hold onto something that you consider a personal territory
or creation, another complication tends to arise—you defend
your possessions.

For a conversational journalism to succeed, the creation of news
and opinion must include the opportunities for community involvement, along with a willingness by journalists to accept and
act on feedback both before *and* after publication or broadcast.
Prior to the publication or broadcast, feedback from the community ought to be sought when possible, particularly from people
quoted or described in stories—and from those who are potentially
affected by the stories. When published or broadcast, should not

major pieces include a profile of the writers and editors responsible—and an invitation to call or write to discuss the story? If the telephone rings constantly, consider the story a catalyst of conversation, even if most of the callers complain or disagree.

At the news organization's end, a positive attitude must prevail, with people who are properly motivated to listen and talk reasonably and receptively. Within newsrooms, a commitment to accuracy must be tempered by the realistic recognition that mistakes in judgment and fact do occur. A well-publicized, accessible system of accountability is needed. Correcting errors or producing follow-up stories that clarify or expand earlier reports will build the community's confidence in the news organization, and upon a bedrock of mutual confidence, communication prospers. To reinforce positive, effective communication attitudes, news organizations might consider a program of internal conversation, stimulated by readings or sensitivity-enhancing experiences, with the talk centering on news and its implications for people.

STORIES THAT EMERGE FROM COMMUNITY

Writing coach Jack Hart (1992) tells a hypothetical story about "journalese":

You finish a long day in the newsroom, head home, and happily detour into the corner tavern. You settle onto a stool, and glance up at the TV flickering behind the bar. On the screen, crowds surge through narrow streets and somber men face one another across large conference tables. The guy hunched over the bar next to you gives you a nudge. "Whaddaya think about all dis?" he asks, his eyes locked on the screen.

You sit up and turn to face him. "Increasingly concerned about Hindu-Moslem violence in the disputed territory of Kashmir, at the border between India and Pakistan, the State Department has moved to expel the leader of a Kashmiri separatist group visiting the United States."

"I'll be damned," he says, pushing his baseball hat back on his head and taking another drag on his Camel. "I never woudda guessed."

You decide to change the subject. "In arguing for passage," you continue, "supporters of the resolution said the availability of health care, including rights to abortion and family-planning services, could have a serious impact on family and work lives of union members."

"Yeah," he says. "I kinda figured that." Then he rises from his stool, slowly pours his beer in your lap and saunters out the door. (p. 26)

Hart exaggerates—to a point—the ways in which journalists talk on the air and in news articles and the reaction they engender. By most accounts, though, news in the form of summary leads and inverted pyramids bores people. The problem is not necessarily the story itself but its presentation. It does not take a readership survey to conclude that people prefer engaging, personalized, and relevant stories (mainly narratives). The alternative journalism connects with people, so it seems, but why? The apparent answer is that it sidesteps the pretense and respects the ability of people to respond. Some alternative news outlets often approximate dialogue and conversation in tone and energy—people talking to people with apparent empathy and understanding.

Norman Sims (1984) has suggested an elixir. He, and others before him, called it "literary journalism," for it combines style and substance in finely crafted stories that touch both emotions and intellect. Such stories are culturally situated, too. Literary journalists, said Sims, report on "the lives of people at work, in love, going about the normal rounds of life. . . . Rather than hanging around the edges of powerful institutions, literary journalists attempt to penetrate the cultures that make institutions work" (p. 3). Sims may have too narrowly defined the work of literary journalists, who can also apply their talents in telling about powerful institutions. The key remains engaging, relevant, and useful journalistic writing which, in the words of Nat Hentoff, "can help break the glass between the reader and the world he lives in" (Schudson, 1978a, p. 187).

The stories Hentoff described can be found in newspapers throughout the country, at least from time to time. They usually take the form of powerful narratives of people confronting the good and, often, the bad of life—AIDS patients, abused children, drug addicts, murder victims. Stories, though, that simply affect our emotions fail to tap the considerable energy they generate; they do not "break the glass." In most cases, emotionally powerful journalism requires information on which people can act—agencies to call, officials to contact, step-by-step procedures to follow explaining how to do this or accomplish that. In other words, it should empower people as active citizens, which increasing numbers of news organizations are now attempting to do.

News on the human condition—on community values and relationships—develops in an evolutionary way. Stories on race relations and sexual harassment, for example, can provoke immediate reactions and responses, but no one expects such problems to disappear as the result of a news report, no matter how compelling it might be. News, though, by traditional definitions, is something fresh, unfolding, and new. That definition—"We did a story on spousal rape last month"—often dissuades news organizations from returning to examine and reexamine enduring conditions, which should be stoked, like the embers in a fireplace, to reignite conversation within the community.

Conversational journalism calls for experimental, even daring, approaches. The experiment might involve using different reporting formats, such as assigning two reporters to cover the same event with each independently producing a published story, followed by an invitation to the people at the events to call or write with their impressions or versions of what transpired. Other experiments might focus on alternative news definitions that lead to stories exploring, for instance, the various aspects of community ethics. Even when reporting so-called hard news stories of violent crime and disturbing, people-against-people behavior, nontraditional approaches can be taken to help community members discuss their feelings, assess their position, and devise an action plan, as the citizens of Dubuque, Iowa, did in devising a plan to entice people of color to move to the community through offers of secure jobs and mortgage and rent subsidies (McCormick & Smith, 1992).

In the well-meaning effort to report evocatively and nontraditionally about the community, journalists must guard, however, against stories that undermine community by reinforcing prevalent images of urban life (rural life, too) as depressing, dangerous, and violent and as filled with dishonest and desperate people. Many news reports, especially those from the police beat, contribute to a victim mentality that leads some people to withdraw from the community and shun others. A 1992 report called "The News as if All People Mattered" concluded that journalistic "reductionism" that explained complex conditions in simplistic terms tended to polarize the community. Commenting on the polarization effect, Betty Friedan (Gersh, 1992) asked whether news organizations had perhaps intensified fears and hatred of people of other races and life-style by focusing on scapegoats for crime, violence, and other social strains rather than the root causes. Certainly, news reports that bombard people daily with dire, upsetting news that is short on context and hope for improvement offer little encouragement for the advancement of community or humanity. When news organizations tell dramatic stories of murders, rapes, robberies, home invasions, and carjackings, and when they produce touching accounts of hunger, illness, discrimination and inhumanity, they should report within a context that explains, assesses, and analyzes: Why the violence; why the suffering? Is this a community in danger or without hope? What can be done?

Geneva Overholser (1991) offered us a concluding thought about news organizations and community: "We need to have a vision of our communities, what they are and what they could be, and the roles we can play in making it come about. . . . Every time we think to ourselves that the political process is leaderless, self-important, risk-averse, colorless, self-perpetuating, pays lip service to change and avoids action on it—we ought to ask ourselves: Is this politics we're describing? Or us?" (p. 38). Journalists ought to ask the people of their communities what they think and what they dream and should then listen widely and attentively. The vision belongs not only to journalists, but to the entire community.

The Listening Role of Journalism: A Place in the Public Conversation

Just when some political commentators were bemoaning the decline of citizen participation in the American democratic process, we gave an election and somebody came. The 1992 presidential campaign rejuvenated a listless electorate. The emergence of H. Ross Perot as a viable third-party candidate and the undeniable economic crisis gripping the country awakened U.S. citizens. Many people began to feel as if they had a personal investment in the campaign and that an outcome beyond business as usual could be expected no matter who captured the presidency or what party gained or lost seats in Congress. However, something else also stirred the public, and that significant development suggests, in part, how journalism might begin to redefine itself.

In Campaign '92, candidates appeared to recognize a need to speak not *to* but *beyond* journalists, and a need to listen not just *to* but *through* them. Journalism became transparent. Perot pledged that if elected he would employ media for shaping government policy around the public sensibility and not the converse; he claimed that media should serve as pipelines informing elected officials of public sentiment. Through "electronic town hall" meetings, politicians would more thoroughly know what citizens prefer and be better able to react to those expectations. Although neither George Bush nor Bill Clinton exercised the electronic town hall metaphor as much as Perot did, their campaign strategies, particularly that of Clinton, persistently appealed to the same wellsprings of citizen participation and voice. Clinton demonstrated two major tactical choices. First, he often assumed the listener role himself, inviting citizens to voice their concerns, and second, he encouraged the public perception of a less visible role for media in the election. One rhetorical event in Clinton's campaign dramatically illustrated the power and implications of such tactics.

THE CLINTON-BROWN DIALOGUE AND THE
PLACE OF THE JOURNALIST

While Clinton and former governor Jerry Brown of California were campaigning for the Democratic party's nomination, and after the campaign had realistically been narrowed to these two candidates, their staffs arranged a joint appearance on "Donahue," the nationally distributed talk show, which typically ranges from light banter on entertaining subjects to serious discussions on public policy issues. Viewers might watch a bikini fashion show one day, only to tune in the next day to find an interview with Henry Kissinger or an exposé of U.S.-backed dictators in Latin America. On April 6, 1992 (because of syndication, the show may have aired on different dates in different markets), Phil Donahue introduced an unusual format for both talk shows and political dialogue: the host would butt out. Clinton and Brown were to discuss their candidacies in the usual "Donahue" show studio, but without the usual studio audience. Instead, they directed their remarks to each other. Donahue sat quietly nearby and only introduced and concluded the program, beginning with, "I am pleased to present Governor Brown, Governor Clinton," and closing with, "Gentlemen, thank you both." Although Donahue left the usual theme music and commercial format of the show unchanged, he took no verbally directive role, even in inserting commercial breaks, which evidently were cued directly to the candidates by the rising volume of theme music.

The structure of this political dialogue was, for a number of reasons, more encouraging than the electronic town hall idea (which poses special problems of mass manipulation) and more promising for journalism than many other developments of this unusual campaign. Despite the fact that the only media representative present, Donahue, had no speaking role and appeared to be superfluous, the Clinton-Brown dialogue in many ways offers almost a prototypical example of the conversation of journalism. Beyond the refreshing novelty of two presidential candidates talking together without interruption or script on national television were the important symbolic dimensions of the meeting, for they can represent—perhaps unwittingly—journalism's emerging conversational role in the public sphere. Consider what happened while Clinton and Brown spoke.

- Donahue remained present in the immediate vicinity of the principals, despite his nonspeaking role—a choice we analyze as the *presence* issue.

- Donahue retained his usual and familiar format for what amounted to an unusual program. At the show's opening, the defining camera angle was to the rear of and above the seated candidates, overlooking the small table separating them, with the host seated several feet away and the empty auditorium behind him. Thereafter, cameras focused on the candidates from Donahue's visual perspective. These decisions, which were made by the show's producers, assumed an atmosphere of context familiarity in what we describe as the *context* issue.

- Donahue provided a forum for the dialogue by introducing the discussion and thanked Brown and Clinton at its conclusion. The *forum* issue involves the crucial functions of sanctioning and sponsorship.

The majority of viewers probably believed that the content of the candidates' talk—what they said—constituted the essential political message of the program. For our purposes, however, it makes more sense to consider the event from a perspective of listening, not speaking. We also consider its implications, not just for campaigning, but for journalism itself as a site or arena for the public drama.

The Presence Issue

Whether you consider Donahue a journalist, a quasi-journalist, or merely an entertainer, his presence alongside Clinton and Brown represented journalism's role and place in the public drama. He sat throughout the meeting as a symbolic public listener, representing visually the public's presence at the conversation. Donahue's presence reassured us that despite his predominant silence, he remained an interested party and, at any moment, was a potential contributor or even an interrupter. Even in his reduced role, Donahue remained a potent force for influencing, and even re-directing, the discussion, if he chose to do so. He further repre-sented public access—a reminder that a public voice, though at times silent, is not to be silenced. This message became much more powerful than if Donahue had chosen to be an aggressive inter-viewer of the candidates. His presence, finally, reminded us of the public's place in the civic conversation: in a democracy, dialogue belongs to the people. It is not to be co-opted or usurped, but should be mediated by journalism.

The Context Issue

Without a large studio audience, the Clinton-Brown conversa-tion could have been televised from a living room or conference room to emphasize the intimacy of the event or the directness of the talk. Instead, Donahue and his producers staged the meeting in a largely deserted theater. The empty seats, in effect, were us; symbolically, the place was packed. To speak meaningfully to each other, Brown and Clinton needed the audience that television provided. Their talk, however interesting to them individually, made no inherent sense outside of a context of listeners interested as they were in comparing the qualities and the words of the candidates. Although the immediate context for the dialogue was *face-to-face interpersonal dialogue*, which meets many of our cultural expectations for the "best" kind of talk, the extended context more realistically could be considered a *faces-to-faces, interpersonally mediated dialogue*. The candidates were acutely aware of the wider audience, even though they appeared to address only one another; lest they momentarily forget, the empty seats and cameras—the normal contextual artifacts of performance, not everyday face-to-face conversation—were there to remind them. The same artifacts stood as reminders of the audience's own importance.

The Forum Issue

The Donahue program clearly served as a vehicle for the presentation of issues and viewpoints, and, as such, resembled in its effect a political advertisement. However, to dismiss the event as a campaign pseudo-event overlooks a crucial facet of the meeting and journalism's potential for affecting the quality of political life in a democracy. Granted, both candidates undoubtedly came to the studio prepared with rehearsed statements they hoped to insert in the conversation. Undoubtedly, too, their handlers had briefed them on what arguments to anticipate and how to answer or refute them. Transcending the competitive element to the talk, however, we find the *forum* function of journalism, in which journalism's most appropriate goal is one of dialogic *sponsorship*. Not only through the "Donahue" program, but in other forums such as presidential and vice presidential debates, journalism properly manages the commons of public ideas when it promotes and enables interaction. In its forum role, journalism goes beyond the mere presentation of each candidate's ideas to the electorate. It explores additional and relevant potential positions raised and explored by dialogue. The central public problem in a democracy is not quite so simple as asking citizens through such forums as electronic town meetings to listen to and evalute political notions; an effective journalism allows the public to listen to ideas tested, at least in part, by their encounter with alternatives provided by journalists or others.

The importance of the Donahue innovation is its symbolic suggestion of a listening role residing at the professional core of journalism. All journalists, whether they are as confrontive as Mike Wallace when he interviews a subject or as unobtrusive as Donahue listening to the Clinton-Brown dialogue, help define the role by their very presence. Some journalists still trust an objective, channel-like or conduit role. Instead, as the Donahue case suggests, journalists act primarily as society's surrogate listeners, and as such, they are inevitably situated within a context *with* speakers. By their presence within that frame, they enable speaking by validating and encouraging—if not always endorsing—the narratives that emerge in public settings. From a communication standpoint, the narrative ("story" in both narrow journalistic parlance and broader social meanings) constitutes as much an emergent construction of listeners as of speakers; it belongs to both, though it is owned by neither.

The listening implications for news organizations challenge the myth that journalists tune in on a story that is already breaking, and then "report" it. Mass communication studies have been bound for too long to a transmission-reception model of communication, which carries the philosophical baggage that reality is a phenomenon "out there" that a perceiver, such as a reporter, does not influence in any direct way. Contemporary cultural studies approaches, however, substitute a reality that is culturally pervasive, consensually shared, and constructed symbolically by all participants. With an altered view of the reality for which journalism is responsible, we can see how the astonishing range of actors, events, and utterances called news is influenced or triggered by the presence (or anticipated presence) of journalistic listeners. From this perspective, a listening role for journalism is more than a mechanical tuning-in; it becomes a sensitive interpretive process by which news people cannot avoid influencing the action by their very presence.

Journalists must (1) be *present* within the news frame, reassuring the public about the potency of its own voice; (2) situate their conventions as part of the symbolic *context* expected by audiences; and (3) appropriately sponsor a *forum* within which issues are interpreted, debated, compared, understood, and ultimately decided. Journalists listen, and by doing so, assist the wider public to listen and evaluate public participation more effectively as well. This, of course, does not mean that journalists should withhold their own ideas from the conversation. However, such contributions must always be in a *listening* context to enable further dialogue. What kind of journalistic listening can best perform this enabling function?

LISTENING AS A WAY OF NEWS: BEYOND THE MEANING-CHOPPER

Loren Reid was a newspaper kid from an earlier era. Because his family owned and operated several small-town weeklies in Missouri and Iowa in the first decades of this century, Reid was born into a milieu of conversation and community that is hard to imagine even in the smallest 1990s town. In his memoir, *Hurry Home Wednesday* (1978), Reid recalled how the Gilman City, Missouri, paper functioned as what his father, only half-jokingly, called "The Great Moral Rejuvenator" or "The Great Moral and Religious Weekly" (p. 36), becoming "a weekly persuader, exhorter, merchandiser, and recorder. One who read it regularly knew the character of the town—its achievements and its hopes" (p. 48). Though some might quibble, it would be difficult to come up with a more succinct statement of newspaper responsibility.

How did such an enterprise work? At its foundation was the most ordinary of human activities, what people in fact do when they simply pass the time together—conversation. Not only was the editor well informed, but he was "sure to engage nearly every business and professional man in serious conversation every week," by selling ads and sensing the news (p. 50). What he missed in those roles he picked up by being the postmaster too, a somewhat more subtle brand of journalism but with roots deep in journalism's history. The key to his success was simple: "Father could get to the bottom of a situation because he was a good listener as well as a good talker" (p. 50). Unfortunately, the contributions of good listening have been neglected for too long when considering the essential core of journalism.

Of course, 1915 is not today, and Gilman City is hardly New York City, Kansas City, or even Iowa City. Reid's father would have more trouble arranging conversations with professionals now in most communities, and he would find that they definitely are not all men any more. Today, he would face even in Gilman City a much more heterogeneous and worldly community, some members of which are in direct and immediate contact with other continents through Internet or other computer bulletin board hookups. He would have more trouble carving a slice out of his own day, too, since his responsibilities as editor would have increased. Moreover, he would find that his readers' interests had exploded (see Wurman, 1990).

One thing has not changed, however; journalists still need to divide their careful attention between both sides of conversational discourse, planning how they listen just as carefully as how they plan to print or broadcast the news. Through listening, journalists discover the events and claims that deserve public attention, learn what various publics want and need to hear and read, discover the appropriate contexts without which any message would be unintelligible, and discover how other journalistic venues are accomplishing similar tasks.

Literary scholar Wayne Booth (1988) once explored the art of listening in a lecture to 600 University of Chicago students at an orientation convocation. He challenged his audience of bright young listeners to read a political essay or hear a political speech and write a summary that the author "would accept as a genuine recovery of his meanings." Booth told the students that he "had no doubt whatever that you could write colorful *criticisms* of what you *thought* he [the politician] said, criticisms that would pass for relevant because they would not miss the target any further than most of what gets printed these days" (p. 183, emphasis in original). Booth then offered cash to anyone who could write a 100- to 250-word summary that could convince Booth that he had been understood in his own speech. To Booth's surprise and satisfaction, three students (one who received a first prize of $25 and two runner-up prizes of $5 apiece) won his little contest. Booth regarded three winners as a small victory against the "great, garbling meaning-chopper that often seems to swallow all our meanings at one end and spew out nonsense at the other" (p. 184).

Which profession did Booth most identify with the insidious, but not always malicious, meaning-chopper? He worried that journalists lack the listening and reading skills to understand the complexities of messages in the public arena. He further worried that journalists fail to understand that in any listening- or reading-related activity, messages are merely *available* to be received. Instead of literally *accepting* the text, a listener or reader must *approach* and question the text with skills and insights that at least correspond to the skills and insights demanded by that text. No content is understood in any significant sense unless the listener carefully and sensitively considers and questions it, at least in part, on its own terms, and does so with skills that help him or her interpret its value. Financially savvy readers find the *Wall Street Journal* interesting partly because they have become adequate to the demands of its stories, while many readers who have not taken the trouble to prepare themselves for its level and kind of journalism are bored, baffled, or both.

As Booth put it, any conversationalist is a kind of journalist: "In our terms, the 'average reporter,' whether a professional reporting for other readers, or simply you and I trying to record for our own future needs, is not free to recover meanings that are richer than his own mind. And the first goal of education is thus to prepare your minds for the free conversation with other minds that can only take place if you really know what those other minds are offering"

(p. 184). A prime requisite for listening, then, is knowledge of and ability to participate within the code or, as Schumacher (1977) once analyzed it, *adaequatio*. Adaequatio is the capacity of a listener or critic to become adequate to the demands of a message, whether the message is musical, visual, or linguistic. Any message for which a listener does not have the tools or language (or interest or will) to interpret might easily be dismissed as worthless gibberish. In fact, this happens embarrassingly often, even to some reporters who should know better, giving rise to statements such as "Symphonies are boring—they all sound the same" or "Psychoanalysis is pure magic and superstition." When asked to write a human interest story about a conductor or a new therapy, can the reporter transcend personal listening limitations, or will the resulting story—no matter how well written—have gone through the meaning-chopper? In practical terms, the limitations of any system of shared information become the limitations of key listeners within the system. "Eloquent" speeches and "inspiring" public figures can truly become eloquent or inspiring only when they are heard or read effectively.

The deceptively simple and straightforward task of listening was long taken for granted, even in the communication sciences. When it was noted and researched at all, it was presumably a matter to be almost entirely judged by the accuracy or fidelity of message reception, as Booth undoubtedly judged his own "recovery-of-meanings" contest. For example, in the classic information theory model of Shannon and Weaver (1949), a viewpoint that influenced communication studies for decades, effective communication was assumed to be the reception and decoding at point B of the message encoded at point A, with as little distortion by "noise" or interference as possible. Although no channel could be expected to eliminate noise entirely, the goal of accuracy seemed clear enough and worthy enough. It is easy to understand how the receiver's role came to be equated with listening. Nothing is wrong with attempting to listen accurately.

However, the accuracy-based receptive approach, while often the first (or only) one that comes to mind, defines at best only a partial view of listening. Journalists also need to understand that listeners and speakers (by which we also obviously mean readers and writers) are inextricably tied together by their *mutual* influences. In practice, this means that we cannot assume this tidy linear sequence: news events happen → journalism attends to events → journalism reports events → public hears or reads about events.

Consider, instead, that many public events in the media world would never happen if journalists were absent—and many seem inevitable any time journalists are present (press agents for celebrities understand this very well). A news reporter conducting an interview with a politician, for example, will find that certain topics and language choices are much more likely to arise in this context than in the politician's interviews with entertainment magazine reporters. Seasoned interviewers also know that just because a source has refused to talk about a subject it does not mean that he or she *will not talk*—it could only mean that the interviewee does not feel comfortable discussing the subject with a given interviewer. In other words, the refusal was not an action that could be understood apart from the context of an interviewer-interviewee system. Seasoned interviewers understand, too, that with some sources, questions and responses come easily, while with others the labored conversation makes it tough to come up with the next comment or probe. These examples provide an analogue to the overall role of journalism and, in fact, a basic truth about communication in general: communication is not merely a transmission-reception phenomenon, but a complex interweaving of mutual influences, many of which are never formally or consciously acknowledged. A journalism that misses this elemental fact is a profession that forever risks blaming others for its own failings, a profession that perpetually wishes others would be different when, in fact, they *would* be different were it not for the journalists.

Without such a recognition, the journalist could write that a mayor "is" a likable, vigorous, and active public speaker, assuming that the mayor's observed actions (when reporters are around) represent his or her typical, everyday behaviors, while in reality, when reporters are not present, the mayor is steely-eyed and dull as dirt. Without a recognition of communication's mutual influences, the journalist might assume that someone is nervous when talking about his or her family, assuming that the topic influences the person's feelings. When a different, perhaps more empathic, interviewer asks about the family, however, the respondent may expand comfortably about his or her feelings, proving that it was not the topic alone but also the particular listener's style that combined with other factors in the communication system to produce the given result.

A TRANSACTIONAL SENSIBILITY

Dewey and Bentley's (1949) notion of *transaction* can help explain the complexity of listening. Many processes in life, they said, cannot be understood except by reference to complementary processes. As they put it, "In ordinary behavior, in what sense can we examine a talking unless we bring a hearing along with it into account? Or a writing without a reading? Or a buying without a selling? Or a supply without a demand? . . . We can, of course, detach any portion of a transaction that we wish, and secure provisional descriptions and partial reports. But all this must be subject to the wider observation of the full process" (pp. 133–134). In other words, speaking should be understood in terms of what it implies—the presence of listeners. Listening becomes part of the definition of the speaking process and speaking becomes part of the definition of listening. To consider speaking (or listening) as separate from its counterpart is to divide the world artificially and unnaturally into components and, as Dewey and Bentley claimed, lose our ability to understand the "full process."

Transactional philosophy recognizes that the world is connected in myriad ways that are not always obvious on the surface. A sensitivity to transaction is a more subtle—and, ultimately, more practical—way to view communication. It revises the overly simplistic assumptions of cause and effect. For instance, journalists do not "cause" readers and viewers to become disillusioned with politics in this view, and public expectations will not "cause" journalists to become image-oriented. Instead, transactionally speaking, how each side defines its role helps shape how the other defines its role. Realities are interdependent.

Nonetheless, journalists often seek easily packageable insights or answers. By persistently listening for simple cause-and-effect answers, they model a world that inaccurately reflects the complexity of social life and, unwittingly, they encourage simplistic cause-and-effect rhetoric from public figures. Such behavior can be more than annoying; it may explain why public figures often feel inadequately understood by "the media." If journalism refuses to listen transactionally, it begins to supply its own answers or, perhaps just as dangerous, begins merely to echo prepackaged answers of public relations spokespersons for companies, agencies, or candidates, who are charged with putting the most pleasant coherent face on ambiguous situations.

A transactional sensibility for journalism, we believe, must imply three things: listening must be emphasized as a fundamentally interpretive activity, it must be characterized by both *doubting* and *believing*, and journalistic listening must—in ways that are currently atypical—come to fuel rather than quell public dialogue. Let us consider these changes in turn.

First, journalistic listeners should understand that listening is interpretive, not simply receptive. Of course, in any interchange, communicative fidelity will be important. If the interviewee says, "I had nothing to do with that particular trust fund," the journalist who writes in his or her notes, "I had not thought about that particular trust fund," clearly has not listened effectively at the level of reception. At this most basic level, listening improvement involves the skill of decoding messages more accurately; it involves the physiological process of hearing. But in communication and psychological research, what is usually considered listening is more psychological than physiological. It takes into account the listener's unique interpretations and attempts to make sense out of the language chosen by the speaker (Wolvin & Coakley, 1991). Every listener does so in a different manner, sometimes so different as to convince speakers that listeners to their words must have heard different statements, or must be fantasizing, or must be lying. However, according to Jerome Bruner (1986), among the most noted psychologists of our century, "We know the world in different ways, from different stances, and each of the ways in which we know it produces different structures or representations, or, indeed, 'realities'" (p. 109). He found that "a generation of research" supports the view that "each mode of representing the world carries with it a prescription as to what is 'acceptable' as input: experience, so to speak, is not 'theory-independent.'. . . [and] there is no seeing without looking, no hearing without listening, and both looking and listening are shaped by expectancy, stance, and intention" (pp. 109–110).

Journalistic listeners inevitably approach their materials interpretively and just as inevitably are coshapers of their messages, which they believe they are merely "objectively receiving." A more conscious recognition of this concept, along with professional listening skills training that supports it, would be an important step in implementing a public conversation *of* journalism and improving the public conversation *about* journalism.

The second transactional change that we recommend for journalists is to give equal weight to what Peter Elbow (1973, pp. 147–191) called the *doubting game* and the *believing game*. Elbow believed that these two metaphors accurately capture persons' attitudes about investigating the world in which we live, as well as some implicit "rules" by which they behave. The doubting game, according to Elbow, fuels much of our contemporary society; it is the basis of most of traditional scientific discovery and much of adversary journalism, for that matter. The person who plays the doubting game appears to say "So what?" "Prove it to me," or "I don't think you're right—persuade me." One can imagine many instances in which this is an extremely pragmatic attitude; we hope the U.S. Food and Drug Administration, for example, plays the doubting game when companies want to market new food additives and prescription drugs. Nothing is inherently wrong with the doubting game—unless it is the only game you know how to play.

Unfortunately, although most journalists in our experience are sensitive and caring people, many have adopted a variant of the doubting game as their sole professional self-image, their basic professional role. The doubting game in journalism can take two forms: the objective, "clean slate" reporter, and the watchdog reporter. The clean-slate reporter in effect says: "You tell me what you want to tell me—I'll look for your flaws of reasoning and question you when you don't make sense." The watchdog reporter seems to say, "If I don't act as the watchdog for City Hall, who will? I have to doubt and question the mayor on everything. If I appear to be on her side, people will think I've been co-opted."

The journalist enacting the believing game, in contrast, temporarily "suspends disbelief" while listening and observing, "giving the benefit of the doubt" to the other communicator. Such a listener understands the value of assuming that reality really might seem quite sensible and meaningful from "over there," in the experience of the other person. Such a listener does not dismiss messages too readily as "stupid," "self-serving," "crass," or "mere propaganda." Such a listener is ready to believe, while listening, that the words uttered by the other person might not seem like stupid, self-serving, propagandistic pap to the other person, or to his or her supporters, or within his or her organizations or culture. The long-standing antagonism between some reporters and public relations specialists is a case in point. Although many public relations professionals have a knack for getting their messages in the media, journalists often presume that those messages are biased, misleading, or untrue by the very nature of the profession. Therefore, they feel, anything coming from a PR professional should be regarded with automatic cynicism. This propensity for doubting, as perceived by the other "side," sets up the very attitude by which slanted PR messages are more likely to be seen by the PR specialist as necessary to penetrate the bias of news journalists. The same could be said of politicians and others who are experienced in dealing with a doubting press. The mutual perceptions of doubt create a vicious cycle of mistrust in which the public can be the major loser.

Journalists who play the believing game need not renounce doubting, but at times they should temper it with empathy and identification. The major justification for this deference is simple fairness. Journalists never know when their biases are unnecessarily clouding or blocking mutual understanding and, as we have suggested, listeners are just as integral to the communication process as speakers. A second justification is purely pragmatic—people trust and talk more to listeners who they believe are making a good-faith effort to understand their perspectives. *Believing* in the sense that we intend it here does not necessarily imply agreement or the phony or artificial means by which some journalists deceptively suggest to an interviewee, for example, that "I'm on your side." A journalist need not be an accomplice to give a full hearing, even to an accused murderer.

As the third transactional change, we recommend that journalists continually remind themselves of their responsibilities to fuel public dialogue. Renouncing simplistic solutions of "right" and "wrong," can journalists trust that they are not the only ones intelligent and capable enough to render judgments about public life? Journalism must recognize its interpretive and critical role yet strive to fulfill its forum functions. One simple and direct pathway to this goal is for each journalist, when considering and planning interviews, to be alert to these kinds of questions:

- Will my story give other potential listeners fair and reasonable access to this person's—or this group's—ideas and motivations? That is, will I increase or maintain my audience's freedom of interpretation relative to these ideas, or will I artificially decrease it?

- Will my story provide enough context for this person's remarks that my own readers or listeners will be able to discuss them intelligently?

- Will my story clearly compare this person's perspectives to the other relevant perspectives within the same topic area or sphere of discussion?

- Will my story acknowledge in some way that my presence was at least a partial determinant of this person's messages?

- Will my story invite others who are now silent to react, testing their voices by entering the public conversation?

- Will my story potentially start more conversations than it stifles, perhaps even stimulating more productive arguments than it settles?

Of course, not all stories are appropriate places to start arguments or invite the voiceless into public life. However, if journalists keep such questions in the forefront of consciousness, public dialogue will be immeasurably invigorated. The answers to some questions on the checklist may necessarily be "no," but the prospect of a "no" at times does not—and cannot—invalidate asking such questions in the first place, for the questions reflect a dialogic-value orientation seldom found in current journalistic practice, especially in the United States.

Journalism's failure to assert itself as a catalyst of civic conversation might explain how influential political philosopher James Fishkin could write an entire book (1992) on the subject of improving public dialogue, yet include no sustained discussion of the role of news media in his scheme. No entry appears for "journalism" in his index, and under "mass communication," a notation says, "See Communications Technology" (three entries). Although Fishkin's book is not critical of journalism and media policies, he evidently fails to see journalism as a locus of change for either stimulating or elevating political dialogue. If true, an explanation might be found in two articles by Daniel C. Hallin (1992a, 1992b). Hallin believed that many journalists "are too constrained by the need to avoid offense to any major political faction or, most powerfully, to the majority sentiment of the moment. In the case of elections, . . . journalists tend to steer the discussion in the direction of technical questions that don't seem political: Which candidate is running the most effective campaign?" (1992a, p. 20). Economic and political forces thus maneuver journalists into a peripheral role of neutral mediation.

Hallin articulately discussed two conclusions about the political implications of journalism's responsibilities when faced with "the emptiness of the American public sphere": first, "journalists need to move from conceiving their role in terms of mediating between political authorities and the mass public, to thinking of it also as a task of opening up political discussion in a civil society," and second, "it might be time for journalists themselves to rejoin civil society, and to start talking to their readers and viewers as one citizen to another, rather than as experts claiming to be above politics" (1992a, p. 20). Note that although Hallin did not overtly discuss journalism's preferred new role as listening-based, that is a clear implication of his analysis. A journalism that conceives itself only in terms of mediation ends up forgoing any responsibility to listen; it becomes a mere conduit constantly waving its white flag, pleading, "Don't kill the messenger." To open political dialogue is to listen well and carefully for implication and nuance, then skillfully invite response. Only a participative, conversational journalism is up to the task.

A LISTENING JOURNEY AND MISSION

The importance of listening in journalism is obvious. Much of what passes for news these days is interview-driven in that what is said and heard is later reported as the story, with the journalist serving as the vital link between face-to-face discourse and the mass audience. However, too often the "obvious" is not so clear, and journalism is presented to students, professionals, and public alike as "reportage" of "events" by "neutral observers." The connection of journalism with talk, with conversation, and with the basic language by which ordinary folks negotiate their everyday lives is lost. However, without listening at its core—in both the mundane implications of listening in interviewing and its grander metaphorical implications in defining the profession—journalism renders itself expendable.

Bill Moyers introduced his 1971 book, *Listening to America*, with a statement that is at once profound and disturbing in the context of our country's involvement in Vietnam. In 1994 we should be no less impressed by its power and no less disturbed by its implications for day-to-day journalism. Moyers wrote:

> For ten years I listened to America from a distance. As Deputy Director of the Peace Corps, special assistant to the President, and publisher of *Newsday*, I lived and worked on a narrow strip of the Eastern Coast. In Washington I helped to draft legislation which we hoped would make this a better country. In New York I belonged to a profession whose express purpose is to communicate with people. But I learned that it is possible to write bills and publish newspapers without knowing what the country is about or who the people are. Much changed in American in those ten years. There were thirty-five million more of us, we seemed more raucous than ever, and no one could any longer be sure who spoke for whom. I wanted to hear people speak for themselves. In the summer of 1970, carrying a tape recorder and a notebook, I boarded a bus in New York to begin a journey of thirteen thousand miles through America. (1971, p. 1)

A bus ride of 13,000 miles still offers a limited and somewhat distorted view of any country, even geographically, but Moyers was motivated by the same desire that propels us to suggest a transactional listening mission for journalism. Compared with Moyers's 1970 bus ride, our contemporary journey involves a similar reconnection with daily life. Beyond that need to rediscover the people (do we know, for instance, much more now about "who speaks for whom"?), journalists today seem even more obviously called to rediscover themselves and their potential to influence the action in an environment of civil discourse.

We cannot be certain what kind of journalism is needed for any age, yet each age challenges communication professionals to come to grips with change. In our view, journalism, as it is presently defined and practiced, fails to listen well enough to contribute to a public conversation. Clearly, a public that respects dialogue is our best agency for democracy as we rapidly approach the next century.

Newstelling: Once upon a Time in Journalism

> The files in the front office would have you believe the two of them go to the same school and technically speaking, this is correct.
>
> They both walk the same long halls, weaving through the same crush of teen-age bodies. They sit in classrooms only a hundred yards from each other, trapped behind weathered desks scrawled with the same declarations of love and lust. They rail against the same mind-numbing rules, make cracks about the same principal, sneak off the same campus at lunchtime, just to escape whatever's being dished out in the cafeteria.
>
> The truth is, though, the two of them don't go to the same school at all. Even if they brushed shoulders in front of their lockers, they probably wouldn't notice each other. They are invisible to each other.
>
> —T. French, "South of Heaven," May 12–21, 1991

These first three paragraphs in a seven-part series in the *St. Petersburg Times* introduces the lives of several students at a high school in Largo, Florida. "South of Heaven" follows "YY," Mike, and other students through their last year at school. Reporter Tom French uncovered little that most of us would consider "newsworthy"; he found no corruption or wrongdoing, quoted few officials or leaders, and offered no solutions to the problems faced by the education system.

From the perspective of conventional journalism, he had no lead, took too long to get to the point, wrote too much, and essentially had no news. Nonetheless, he ended up with a compelling story that gave many people a rare opportunity to be invited into the incredibly complex lives of high school students. At another level, readers could well have come away from the story with a fuller understanding of the education system, even though that was not directly addressed. In *Times*-sponsored town meetings that grew out of the series, hundreds of community members discussed and debated educational issues. The story has been discussed, reread, studied, reprinted, and rewritten for other media.

That same year, *St. Petersburg Times* reporter Sheryl James wrote "A Gift Abandoned," another extraordinary story. It began:

> That day, Ryan Nawrocki was just an ordinary sixth-grader living an ordinary life. He was 11 years old, with blond hair that hung straight and heavy on his forehead. He was a stocky kid, and it was easy to imagine him carrying a baseball mitt or playing video games after dinner. That day, Thursday, April 27, Ryan strode across the street from his house in Wildwood Acres, a complex of shoe-box-shaped duplexes on streets that curl into other streets lined with more shoe boxes. He headed toward a small courtyard where his 16-year-old sister, Melissa, was doing laundry in a small community building. Walking along a worn foot path, he passed the dumpster and a large oak tree.
>
> He heard something. A kitten? (James, 1991, p. 1)

For years earlier, in Minnesota, Jackie Banaszynski had written "AIDS in the Heartland" for the *St. Paul Pioneer Press Dispatch*.

> Death is no stranger to the heartland. It is as natural as the seasons, as inevitable as farm machinery breaking down and farmers' bodies giving out after too many years of too much work.

But when death comes in the guise of AIDS, it is a disturbingly unfamiliar visitor, one better known in the gay districts and drug houses of the big cities, one that shows no respect for the unusual order of life in the country. The visitor has come to rural Glenwood, Minn. (Banaszynski, 1988, p. 1)

Both James and Banaszynski won Pulitzer prizes. James re-created the circumstances surrounding a mother's abandonment of her baby, and Banaszynski wrote about how two men lived when facing certain death from AIDS.

A security guard sent a letter to the *Pioneer Press Dispatch* saying that each chapter "tore me apart and also gave me a great sense of serenity in how the two dealt with the disease. In all honesty, all three chapters produced tears. . . . I am not touched by a lot of things, but this was so special, writing and story telling at its finest" (Howell, 1988, p. 21).

The three series touched people in many ways and were debated in corner coffee shops and corporate board rooms alike. It was not just the writing, though the writing was good in all three, and it was not just the content. Abandoned babies and death from AIDS are compelling subjects, but French's piece caused quite a stir even though its subject cannot be called sensational.

STORY AND NEWS

Other such stories throughout the country evoke similar responses. In part the response arises from the comparison to conventional journalism, in which news and information relate to the fleeting facts of everyday bureaucratic business; the contrived objectivity of sparse, cool paragraphs, the dry, pedestrian, even rigid form. Story or narrative can "cover" the same information, but usually with an impact that is more lasting, solid, human, warm, full, emotional, creative, round, free. Story touches us in a way that conventional news does not.

Reporting and writing news should be more than covering official actions by quoting official sources. More than that, however, reporting and writing should result in news that is accessible, and even inviting. Conventional news and news forms are quite effective in providing an ordered set of facts, but as citizens, we require more to make sense of ourselves and our relationships in the ever-increasing complexities of our environment. We need narrative forms that not only describe and explain but embrace numerous and diverse perspectives. People use journalistic forms to tame an unpredictable, unruly universe with familiar forms, meanings, and realities. No single form or method exists that can capture or mirror an event, issue, or other "reality." Who is to define such a reality? Even if an official version were defined, a report of it would not create or duplicate the reality. The best journalists can do is report what they learned as completely as possible.

The predominant journalistic form for a century has been the inverted pyramid, which lists facts from most to least important. It is a form that complements a news conventionally defined as timely, accurate facts from official sources. A conventional news report does create order out of disorder, but it reflects a particular order, and its assumptions require particular facts. It is the form of our expectations of news. Other forms, including story, often have different, and lesser, functions. While news is considered information, story is entertainment. The dichotomy between "information" and "entertainment" has been destructive and wasteful, essentially discounting in journalism a powerful form of communication, capable of not only providing an alternative perspective on our world, but also drawing into the social dialogue more participants as both sources and readers. Narrative and story are so deeply rooted in human physical and mental processes (Scholes & Kellogg, 1966; Bruner, 1986, 1990) that such approaches to news are inviting and relevant. The inverted pyramid, because of its ubiquity and association with "serious" news, has become identified as the "natural" way to deliver important, factual information, but story, so much a part of us, is more natural to human communicators.

Narrative and *story* have become more popular journalistic terms in the past few years. We use them interchangeably to mean an ordering of information that results in a story with some kind of beginning, middle, and end. Others have dealt with the complexities of definition (Atkinson, 1990; Cronon, 1992; Scholes, 1966; Cohan & Shires, 1988). Story approaches to news are powerful and potentially rewarding, but define an attitude more than a technique or tool. Story is invitational, not only inviting people to read or receive, but to become part of the story. Story-based reporters, by definition, cannot be arrogant or possessive. They know they do not possess the Truth, to be transmitted to an audience of readers or sold to a consumer market. They know they share something beyond facts gathered daily, the ephemeral flotsam from faceless officials at countless bureaucracies. They know the people who read their stories share those stories, partly as their creators. Stories do not spring up anew from each day's murders, elections, accidents, disasters, corruptions, and triumphs. Details do, and stories feed off facts, creating and recreating themselves, growing up out of the culture, our common depths. They are part of us all, and we are part of them.

That is why virtually anyone who reads "South of Heaven," "A Gift Abandoned," or "AIDS in the Heartland" can find in them fragments of their own lives. We may not be high school students, or parents, or gay, but we identify with such stories because powerful elements in them deeply touch experiences we know and understand. The story transcends its facts, and while we can learn many facts from a story, speakers and listeners participate through story in a deeper cultural experience.

Before newspapers, and even before printing, tellers of tales shared that cultural experience by traveling the countryside narrating stories that became the news. Stories and ballads told of births, deaths, royalty, wars, and odd or unusual happenings. With the rapid spread of printing came broadside ballads, corantos, and other forms radiating many of these same themes and stories from major urban centers to the countryside in areas throughout the world. The content of early newspapers often strongly resembled that of older story forms (Shepherd, 1973).

U.S. papers in the middle to late 1700s and through much of the 1800s frequently cast news as story, which was often about crimes. In the 1800s, writers such as Charles Dickens and Mark Twain wrote engaging news narratives (see Snyder and Morris, 1942, for a collection of such pieces). Dark themes emphasized the depravity of the human soul, the vileness of intemperance, and the wastefulness and stupidity of rash acts, all timeless subjects in their appeal. Often such stories carried a strong sense of justice, a notion strengthened by repetition.

In fact, the repetition of timeless themes seemed an integral part of news as story. With elaborate plot variations, writers urged faith, goodness, frugality, temperance, hard work, hope, and other Christian qualities. Dates, names, and places were often vague or missing, because the emphasis was not on any correspondence between the facts of the story and any outside reality. Instead, the early narrative journalism taught the moral or lesson of the situation. Overt religious references were part of the news in the late 1700s and early 1800s, when a newswriter might declare a particular murder to be an affront of God and might characterize a massacre or natural disaster as divine retribution for sinful, hedonistic ways. Similarly, a drowning or rescue would be termed a providential act. Such references diminished as the nineteenth century progressed; although newspapers still covered religious convocations, dissensions, and changes of leadership, they now reported them as matters of occurrence or fact rather than as value-laden components of a larger story to be shared.

Beginning in the 1830s, newspaper publishers realized that they could make money with facts, particularly those gathered from police and courts. Virtually all early papers included opinion throughout their content, but as their pages bloomed with factual reports, papers began confining opinion to specific columns or pages. As daily distribution replaced weekly publication, notions of time and timeliness in news shifted to briefer units, with the daily, and even hourly, deadline. That shift redefined what constitutes news and newsworthiness. Values seemed far less tangible, and therefore less important than facts, and they were also less marketable. Values were timeless and did not require brand new stories for constant updating. Facts, on the other hand, died with the present story and required daily renewal or resurrection. A fact-based newspaper that created insatiable demands for new articles, events, and people better suited the routines and demands of daily journalism.

After the 1840s, the telegraph, in part because of its unreliability and expense, was used to present facts in order of importance, which is essentially the definition of the now-familiar inverted pyramid format for news. While the telegraph did not invent the form (Mindich, 1993), it removed the opportunities for competing forms, essentially discouraging the tall tale, the hoax, and a lot of irony, satire, and humor (Carey, 1986), which are all part of the language of story.

The inverted pyramid form became associated with truth and fact and came to dominate American journalism. It is perfectly adapted to a fact-based form. As newspapers through the nineteenth century reached more people and made more profit, facts replaced opinion because it became clear that facts were the better product. Facts became commodities, ideally packaged in the inverted pyramid showcase which organized and ordered them to maximum advantage. Because facts became part of the salable news product, reporters sought them out, making them the very definition of journalism. Their form requires factual content, and thereby serves to define what is newsworthy.

A more complex explanation for the triumph of fact comes from considering the advancement and perceived necessity of scientific achievement in many disciplines and professions, including journalism. Science was ruled by truth, fact, and objectivity, realms in which "story" seemed out of place. When the papers told stories to illustrate values, facts seemed less important than morals or lessons. When the papers reported events and happenings as facts and made issues out of fairness, accuracy, and objectivity, facts assumed primary importance. As reporters cited sources and attributed quotes, each citation and quotation became a fact. Journalism's truths became journalism's facts, and accuracy in even the most minute details was now revered. Truth and fact, no matter how narrow, came to drive journalism.

Journalism had created a new audience for fact while depleting, but not submerging completely, the audience for story. The fact-based audience, consistent with a modernist scientific temper, naturally expected that news facts could increase the precision of public knowledge and, therefore, settle disputes, proving that some ideas were better than others. For example, Czitrom (1982) demonstrated that many Americans believed the invention of the telegraph would make war obsolete because people could now communicate their differences directly and precisely. Such naïveté, if it now seems ridiculous, at least points to differences in fact-based and story-based journalism. The *criterion* for the former is accuracy, the *mode* is transmission, and the *purpose* was to conclude—to settle disputes, prove claims, or demonstrate issues. Story-based journalism operates differently. Its *criterion* is the development of shared understanding, its *mode* is conventional dialogue—the mutual involvement of communicators—and its *purpose* is to situate both message senders and receivers within a common temporal or cultural framework for generating meaningful explanations. (In Chapter 5, we discussed this as a phenomenon of community.) This common framework does not mean agreement, artificial or otherwise; in fact, it is only within a story-based journalism that conflicts may be meaningfully addressed, since its purpose is not to prove conclusions or represent reality in some single, "correct" way.

ROOTS OF NARRATIVE COHERENCE IN NEWSTELLING

Stories, of course, have their facts and narrow truths as well, but they operate at other levels. The first stories in prehistory may have come from warnings given to children not to venture too far from caves because of "monsters" or other horrors and from warriors or hunters coming from afield with exaggerated tales of their prowess (Ransome, 1909). Primitive storytellers may have gained a wealth of social advantage, by using stories to explain the mysteries of life and universe, or to express accurately the feelings and relationships listeners had with each other and their environments. Similar functions have been attributed to news (Jensen, 1977, Mead, 1925–1926). Jensen, in fact, called reporters "modern-day medicine men" whose job it is to provide answers to questions (on the deficit, inflation, race relations, etc.) that have no answers. It is possible that the power derived from providing answers and explanations through story may have led to the beginnings of religion, with the storyteller as shaman or spiritual leader. Indeed, Gerbner (1977) has associated television, our most prolific modern-day storyteller, with religion.

Fact and event in news are certainly important, but story-based news emphasizes theme and context. In some cases, the facts, the unusual or unique circumstances, and the individual actors in the story become less significant than the story itself. Once the particulars of any process are perceived in a pattern, the pattern assumes prime importance. That news interests, convinces, or even entertains readers is not necessarily the result of correspondence to an objective reality, although the facade of an empirical truth might be beneficial to news in other ways (Warner, 1959). "Facts" may be ephemeral illustrations of more basic and enduring elements. News researchers (and readers and journalists as well) typically note that news repeats itself; that is, to be a reporter and write news is to find oneself with several forms and many recurring situations. Facts in news are specific and varied, but the forms they fill and the stories they illustrate are more general and less varied.

Considering news as story attributes to the journalist a major responsibility in the creation of the news article. Disseminating news is not a mechanical process controlled by external organizational and bureaucratic elements but a human creation and recreation, a telling and retelling of stories which, at the same time, is the human creation and recreation of reality. To be a journalist is to be a creator. The journalist takes bits and pieces of the world and arranges them into reasonable, coherent narratives. That the world from which these bits and pieces were extracted may be experienced as neither reasonable nor coherent makes the journalist a powerful and important cultural force. Many practitioners neither appreciate the extent to which this is true nor reflect on the context in which it is true.

To begin to consider news in these terms, we need to explore the importance of narrative in ordering our world. We assume that what appears in the newspaper does not correspond exactly with what is called "objective reality." Boulding (1971) saw the world as a swarm of inconsistencies and absurdities that is essentially nonsense, from which people create sense and order. People live in an illusion of order—an order created through constructs such as laws, courts, neighborhood streets, calendars, watches, families, churches, schools, academic departments, and so forth.

Narrative constructs order out of disorder and meaning from meaninglessness. White (1980) argued that reality does not come packaged, as in stories, and that to create narrative sense we must pick and choose from among a myriad of available elements. Narrative, then, as any other potential news form, requires selection; it is a way of seeing the world. In a sense, the human world becomes known through the stories we create to characterize it.

Life, unlike a play, is neither tragic nor comic, happy nor sad, good nor evil. It simply is. Its beginnings, middles, and endings are concocted from ambiguity, and its climaxes and denouements are, at best, relative. Nonetheless, life's temporal and value-laden assortment of thoughts, feelings, actions, and events invites us to make some sense of it. Scholes (1968) said that every time we speak about our existence, we participate in a "taming" activity. Rock (1981) called the "ritualized and cyclical nature of . . . reporting . . . a critical feature of eternal recurrence" of a social order made up of "movement but no innovation" (p. 68). In a grand or overall sense, news, like other narrative forms, is a major ordering activity that seeks to define, explain, report, interpret, and describe the events and happenings of the day.

The result, of course, is a rendering of the event, but not the event itself. Events in the world are not discrete happenings, always obvious and unambiguous in their fits and starts; narrative makes them intelligible. This is at least one area in which journalists and historians find common ground.

History is narrative that usually creates chronological order—from the "discovery" of America to the Declaration of Independence and the Constitution, and so forth. In this way, narrative fashions a particular reality from all the possible realities that can be created; it emphasizes linearity (Ricoeur, 1980; Levi-Strauss, 1963); and it attributes significance to some events while excluding others entirely.

History and news are more than chronological strings of events; as narratives they are sequences in which some events have been accorded increased value or intensity. These concepts roughly parallel Forster's (1927) notions of story and plot. He defines story as the sequence of events (The woman was enraged, then what happened?) and plot as giving meaning to the sequence of events (The woman was enraged, why?). First, we have a narrative or story creating order out of disorder—a human being chooses from any number of events (sequential or simultaneous) and orders them into a sense-making pattern. Second, by making those choices, the human being endows the chosen events with a significance they might not have as part of a mere sequence. History and news are quite similar in these respects. Both create what some would argue is an artificial order and intensity.

Also speaking of history, Munz (1977, p. 240) claimed that although each story has a beginning, it is not *the* beginning, but just a point people might think is a good beginning: "The story must make sense. . . . The reader must be made to feel that there is a beginning and an end and he must be made to feel that once the story has started, one thing follows another with a certain necessity. The sense of a beginning and an ending gives a story coherence, and so does the feeling that the sequence of events is not entirely unpredictable. Given the beginning, one thing led to another and led, through some kind of inherent necessity, to the end" (p. 232).

Neither history nor news is necessarily predictable, and stories need predictability. It would be difficult to build a story of inherent necessity with unpredictable events "if to write a narrative were to copy what happened" (p. 232).

Human beings need such forms to tell what they know, often in such a way that it can be understood across time and space. We understand and learn from many ancient stories, legends, and myths today, no matter where they originated. Story is unavoidable in relating real events, because listeners and readers require a coherence, integrity, fullness, and closure that are not possible outside the telling of a story (White, 1980, p. 23). Accepting this, even news articles often conform in curious, if unplanned, ways: "[As stories they] must arouse and hold the interest of . . . readers. . . . There must be villains and heroes in every paper, and the story lines must conform to the usage of suspense, conflict, the defeat of evil, and the triumph of good that have guided the good sense and artistry of past storytellers and controlled their audience's ability to respond" (Warner, 1976, p. 206).

Stories are about people and their motivations—heroes and villains, good actions and bad actions. Burke (1991) and other historians have argued that such an approach emphasizes events and issues of short duration as opposed to relationships and issues of long duration. While that might be merely uncomfortable for news as it has been conventionally defined, it is disastrous for history. The impetus for social and cultural movement, explanations for long-standing problems such as racial and ethnic prejudice, why certain peoples have various beliefs or worship particular gods, migration and immigration patterns, and many other developments can be illustrated, but not necessarily explained, through stories about people. These explanations require analyses that transcend story forms, or they require story and narrative forms supplemented by analysis and commentary.

Burke (1991) suggested that historians look to literary examples for innovative narrative approaches that overcome some of the problems of a traditional story perspective. Writers could incorporate multiple viewponts, make themselves more visible in narratives to illustrate that their viewpoint is one of several, and make narratives "thick" enough (Geertz, 1973) with detailed description, analysis, and interpretation to deal with structures or long-term relationships, modes of thought and institutions. Some of these approaches have been incorporated in a work by Schama (1991). While journalism's narratives, including "South of Heaven" (French, 1991) and the others mentioned earlier, may differ in terms of goals, functions, and perspectives from those of history, journalists can move beyond the "covering" of daily events and short-term issues. French's work, and the work of other journalists, demonstrates that narrative journalism can emphasize lives other than those of officials and leaders and can blend short-term events and issues with broader structures or relationships to describe, explain, and even analyze. Moreover, such stories are appealing and inviting, and they can contribute to a community conversation that leads to debate and, eventually, action.

The story approach does not solve the problems of news. In any article or tale, information and story are torn out of one natural context and placed in another. The content is, in a sense, removed from one world and placed in another; it is removed from the everyday world and placed in the world of mass media. Journalists create this second world, and often, they and the public who depend on the media confuse the two.

This confusion does not mean that these worlds exist independently, each in a vacuum. They share complex interrelationships, which are suggested in most theories of mass communication and news. News stories cannot be created only by so-called sources and newsworkers in isolation; they are created only in a cultural context, and the creation of news requires the participation of an entire culture. Neither sources nor journalists are independent of the cultures within which they live and work, and journalists cannot create a news that is independent of its cultural environment; they cannot erase their own cultural biases from their production of news. This complex interdependence keeps news from being merely information transmitted to a more or less anonymous and unconnected audience. Through the culture they share with the sources and creators of news, people in that audience are already part of the news before it is written and published.

News shares characteristics with oral literature, myth, traditional tales, ballads, literature, family histories, and other forms of cultural narrative. This view of news content as a cultural document in which people create shared meanings shifts the emphasis from news as isolated segments of the day's realities. Rather, news can be considered significant in part because in creating realities, it creates order, and further, this particular kind of ordering can be seen, like literature and myth, as a cultural activity with its own history.

When social critics observe that people in the United States demand solutions, even simplistic ones; that they want to know causes or who or what is to blame, they are saying essentially that people crave the story form, desiring a plot with a beginning, middle, and especially an ending.

INFORMATION, ENTERTAINMENT, AND THE REEMERGENCE OF STORY

News does not always provide stories in simple, traditional forms. The story as a news form diminished after the middle 1800s, but its demise, or relegation to the lesser functions of entertainment, has been exaggerated. Three levels of story can be distinguished in the news: individual article, social theme, and cultural theme. Articles are occasionally stories in themselves, very much in the traditional sense, with beginnings, middles, ends, and the equivalent of plots and characterization. These tend to be told by a single voice. At a second level, families of news articles, not necessarily like traditional stories individually, often tell a story over time. These, as in coverage of a natural disaster like Hurricane Andrew in 1992 or a human-made one such as the siege, attack, and 1993 burning of a cult compound in Waco, Texas, are less likely told by a single voice. At a third level, how culture patterns its news can be seen as its own tale, its story, in which human beings, by giving meaning to some part of their existence, have symbolically created their realities. The whole cultural body of news is told by many voices in many ways, and it represents the ever-continuing conversation of news interpretations and reactions. This conversation constitutes one of the many webs of significance (Geertz, 1973) that we spin as human beings.

Narrative approaches to news, however, became suspect in part because of the emergence of the inverted pyramid and fact-based journalism. News and news forms are often perceived and studied as almost mutually exclusive dualities. Journalists almost always conceive of news articles as discrete elements, either "information" or "story," with the content fact-oriented for information or story-oriented for entertainment. Schudson (1978a) and other scholars have described the splintering of 1880s newspapers into information and entertainment forms. The report in papers such as the *New York Times* came to be identified with fact and information, resulting in "hard" or serious news, while the story/narrative in such papers as the *New York Daily News* came to be identified with sensationalism and amusement, amounting to "soft" or frivolous news.

Some argue that information papers are interested in fact and truth, and entertainment papers, in story and play. Eason (1981) put it this way: "If the emphasis is placed on the relationship of the report to the event, we speak of an informational model of journalism. If the emphasis is placed on the relationship of the report to the reader, we speak of a story model of journalism" (p. 128). The informational model traditionally deals with serious subjects and is judged on accuracy and objectivity, while the story model, which can deal with less serious subjects, is judged primarily on aesthetic criteria.

Roshco (1975), in analyzing the information side of news, found it to be a "necessary, and therefore valuable commodity of social exchange" (p. 10). Hughes (1968), in almost exclusively analyzing the "story" side of news, found it entirely involving what she called "human interest" and valuable almost solely as entertainment. Schudson (1978a) and Gans (1979) called news "important" and story "interesting."

The news/entertainment split can be seen as a manifestation of the ancient contest among *logos* (as philosophic or technical expression), *mythos* (as artistic or aesthetic expression), and *rhetoric* (as persuasion, logic, argument), as to which most accurately, or appropriately, represents truth, knowledge, and reality. Each of these, in various configurations, has been both supported and condemned by significant thinkers throughout history (Fisher, 1985). Prior to Plato's arguments that philosophical discourse was superior to other expressions, logos and mythos were not separate; the philosophic and aesthetic were melded, and as they were not distinct, neither could be said to offer a clearer way to truth and knowledge. Fisher argued that once distinctions emerged, the three forms were driven further apart by arguments as to their potential to deliver truth. Whatever the cause, artistic and intellectual sensibilities are often separated and set against each other. It has been difficult to sustain an argument that any one form is best to embody truth and knowledge. In fact, it might be argued, the original logos, before philosophy, aesthetics, and rhetoric were separated, is most conducive to seeking truth and knowledge. Fisher (1985) argued that the strengths of the three forms are embodied in what he calls the *narrative paradigm*: "[It] sees people as storytellers—authors and co-authors who creatively read and evaluate the texts of life and literature. It envisions existing institutions as providing "plots" that are always in the process of re-creation rather than as scripts; it stresses that people are all participants in the making of messages, whether they are agents (authors) or audience members (co-authors)" (p. 86).

Burke (1991) reached a parallel conclusion in attempting to accommodate "informational" and "story" forms in history, suggesting a narrative form that included analysis. Dewey (1927), in discussing the need for a more scientific or informational news, argued that it must be presented in artistic fashion. He considered such a marriage ideal.

Narrative writing in journalism makes readers part of the story in ways that other journalistic forms do not. Likewise, stories are pre-embedded in the culture in a way that other journalistic forms are not. Stories are part of our being; we are creatures of narrative, and we live our lives in and by stories. Moreover, we make stories out of bits and pieces of information that come to us in various ways, including the inverted pyramid, headlines, cutlines, captions, bulletins, and other such journalistic forms. Journalists can take great advantage of this part of human nature; they can share their information, and our information, in ancient forms that include all of us as part of a common culture.

Fisher (1985) claimed that the centuries-long struggle among proponents for various epistemological forms resulted in a number of evils, including the "rendering [of] personal and public decision-making and action subservient to 'experts' in knowledge, truth, and reality, and [the] elevating [of] one class of persons and their discourse over others" (p. 87). This can be seen in any newspaper, where the majority of sources on any day are officials, politicians, leaders, and spokespersons of acknowledged authority and access to technical information. Circumstantial evidence, at least, indicates (see Dardenne, 1990) that the rise in use of official sources in newspapers roughly corresponds with an increased use of the inverted pyramid and a decreased use of story.

The point here is not to prove these relationships but rather to note that story-based forms of news which are closely associated with the soft news and entertainment side of journalism are less likely to have official sources, cite experts, or systematically elevate one class over another. They are more likely, in fact, to be representative of a broader range of people than report forms. Reports, and particularly the inverted pyramid, are closely associated with hard news and the information side of journalism, and they are more likely to have official sources and experts. In other words, reports tend to be socially exclusive, while stories are inclusive. People do not just tell and hear stories; they exist together within them.

Critics and practitioners over the years have perpetuated the split among journalistic forms, generally assigning the highest motives and achievements—edification and information—to the report form, and the lowest—entertainment and amusement—to the story. The result has been to drive the practice and practitioners of journalism into a strained and misleading dichotomy, in which not all the profession supposedly trades in truth and information. Many feature writers are respected as making significant contributions to journalism, but mostly they are relegated to lesser status, as are their articles.

Because of this split, journalism is not whole, nor are many journalists. Even labels tell us something about expectations. A news-side "reporter" gets information from people and events deemed important and is often confined to "news forms" that project the image of objectivity, trust, and no-nonsense information. Emphasis for the feature "writer," on the other hand, is placed on style, insight, eloquence, and aesthetics, not so much on straight reporting. Features and other "soft-news" stories traditionally have been relegated to special pages of the paper, usually an inside section devoid of "hard news," although there are certainly notable exceptions to this pattern.

Most news critics see news as timely information, and they see the "information" news as a representation or reflection of some discrete outside reality. Gans (1979) defined "important" news in terms of such news judgments as the importance of subject matter according to rank in governmental and other hierarchies, impact on the nation and national interest, impact on large numbers of people, and significance for past and future. His definition of "interesting" stories reflects the relegation of story to more frivolous, peripheral, and entertaining matters. "Interesting" stories involve people, role reversal, human-interest, expose, anecdote, hero, and "gee-whiz" (p. 156). His definitions clearly separate "news" and "story," assigning important matters to news and the more frivolous, peripheral, "entertaining" matters to story.

Hughes (1968), although she maintained the news/story split, understood that modern news articles have roots reaching deep into the past and that they are not necessarily isolated fragments of information. Darnton (1975), in the brief memoir of his days at the *New York Times*, also emphasized the significance of the historical roots of news. "Of course," he says, "we did not suspect that cultural determinants were shaping the way we wrote about crimes in Newark, but we did not sit down at our typewriters with our minds a *tabula rasa*. Because of our tendency to see immediate events rather than long-term processes, we were blind to the archaic elements in journalism. But our very conception of 'news' resulted from ancient ways of telling stories" (p. 191).

Proponents of the New Journalism have written about real people and events deliberately using literary "devices" (Wolfe, 1973). More critics have analyzed the literary than the traditionally journalistic aspects of this writing. New Journalism supposedly revitalized reporting as a form of storytelling, focusing on events as symbolic of some deeper cultural ideology or mythology, emphasizing the world view of the individual or group, and concentrating on the aesthetics of the reporting process in creating texts that read like short stories or novels (Eason, 1984), but not without the accompanying risk that literary license might lead to justifiable criticism and even legal action.

None of this is to suggest that researchers have overlooked news in ways other than as information and story models, or as transmitted information, or as the result of organizational, societal, and other activities, routines, or processes. Gerbner, in various studies, considered news as a new state religion (1977) and as a highly symbolic form of storytelling (1974). He understood that most of what people know or think they know comes, not from direct experience, but from stories they share through the mass media. Stephens (1988), taking a long-term perspective, traced the origins of news back to ancient times, showing that basic topics of news accounts and general standards of newsworthiness have varied little since ancient times. He argued that "humans have exchanged a similar mix of news with a consistency throughout history and across cultures that makes interest in this news seem inevitable, if not innate" (p. 34). Moreover, he thought that a great attraction of news was its "seemingly inexhaustible supply of tales with which we can delight and divert each other" (p. 17).

Although Europeans have shown more interest in the linguistic, semiotic, cultural, and ideological analysis in news texts than their

American counterparts (see, for example, Cohen & Young, 1981; Glasgow University Media Group, 1976, 1980; Downing, 1980; Fowler et al., 1979), most academic analyses reflect a view of news that Phillips (1976) described as a collection of fragmented, disconnected, discrete, and isolated "facts" or pieces of information. Many aspects of the production and presentation of newspaper news encourage this perception of news as fragmented—from the distinct areas of coverage known as "beats" to the distinct sections and subsections of the published newspaper. It is a perspective supported by tradition, conventions, routines, organization, and socialization.

Broader views of news have been promoted by various scholars, including Carey (1975), who have argued for a "ritual view of communication" in which news is seen in its ability to maintain, and even celebrate, culture. Such views raise the possibility that the function of news is not only to inform, but to maintain—not just to transmit new information for the creation of new views, but to share new information to reinforce and recreate that which we already know. In a compatible view, Stephenson suggested in a theory of reading (1964) and a play theory of mass communication (1967), that news goes beyond a mere transmission of information to serve as play activity or ritual game that maintains and perhaps comforts as much as it informs.

Despite the information/entertainment dichotomy, story is durable and ingrained in all journalism. Articles even in the most information-oriented dailies eventually form stories over time, although fact- and report-oriented, informational newspapers are deemed more important and trustworthy than story- and entertainment-oriented ones. What's more, the term "story" remains associated with falsehood, as in how a child might report a lie told by a classmate, "He told a story." Scientists, doctors, and others provide results of their research and other professional and academic endeavors in the form of reports, not stories. In most news outlets, the story or narrative is used for pieces for which the purpose is not foremost to impart knowledge or provide information, but to entertain, illustrate, distract, or amuse.

News is not just information and entertainment, but through its content and form, as well as through the creating and reading of it, news becomes a recognition of people's connectedness, their societies, and their cultures. It is both specific and universal, both timely and timeless. The "facts" of course are important, but it is also important to discover and explore the whole other story dimension of news. Hughes (1968) said of this: "This newspaper literature—the original stories and the variations on their themes which are printed every day—has the property of viability. Though they make news, which is perishable, they have for the readers the timeless interest of literature" (p. 209).

By emphasizing timeliness, proximity, importance, and other such characteristics, news organizations tend to ignore and even deny the natural and universal part of news. Researchers, readers, and journalists concentrate on facts and relationships to "reality," whatever they might be, encouraging, even rewarding, thinking that leads to a widening gap between "information" and "entertainment" as if the two were different processes.

In doing so, they perpetuate and enforce notions that facts provide information and stories provide entertainment. Consequently, it is more difficult to remind ourselves that stories also provide information, and valuable context—that stories can be taken more seriously. Serious journalists, researchers, and readers who abandon the story form to superficial entertainment use, such as television shows that build sensational stories around crime, debauchery, and human misery, contribute indirectly to a debasement of narrative journalism. Hence, the emergence and dominance of television shows that build sensational stories around crime, debauchery, and human misery—often in ways that reflect badly on more serious forms of journalism. By relating story to sensationalism, or by undervaluing and misinterpreting the sensational nature of story (Bird & Dardenne, 1990), legitimate news organizations have allowed others to co-opt this most culturally powerful and communal news form.

We have to stop considering news in a dichotomy of entertainment or information and as isolated, timely bits of information. We should consider more often its wholeness, its contribution to conversation in which we tell each other stories to entertain informatively and inform entertainingly. The public maintains common access to this conversation, and journalists must revolutionize their ideas and their approaches to invite it. To entertain is to encourage enjoyment, but another connotation of "entertain" suggests also a more conversational mode: When we say we will "entertain" a motion to adjourn a meeting, or that someone "entertains" new ideas easily, we mean that one's attitude is invitational, open to new action and thoughts. A responsible entertainment journalism, though usually considered in the first, almost escapist, sense, may in the long run serve society best when it serves in the second sense.

STORY AND THE PUBLIC

News, clearly, is a far more complex function than conveying fragments of information that live and die in the course of a day's newsprint. Like the stories of ancient storytellers, newspaper and other news content is more than the creation of a single reporter or news organization; it is a joint creation of the tellers and the told. Its traditional forms and contents require the participation of both the people who create and produce the news content as well as the audience that interacts with that content to help order its world and create its realities.

Considering news as narrative or story does not mean it is irrelevant to consider how news corresponds with some reality, how it affects or is affected by society, or how it is a product of journalists or bureaucratic organization, but it does introduce another perspective, one in which news stories transcend their traditional functions of announcing the events of the day.

News, when considered as story and conversation, is more an attitude than a technique. While it can be argued that news articles and all of news eventually constitute stories, a news-as-story approach allows people to explore more consciously other ways of seeing. We may, for example, more constructively revisit Park's

(1944) statement that news does not so much inform as orient. By orienting, news helps us establish relationships with each other and our environment. Informing may be seen as more of a competitive, even alienating function—we use news to gather facts, to compile or amass, and to arm ourselves. Orienting is more of a community-linking function—we use news to find our commonalities and differences, to draw together and discuss. News is not simply the reporting of the day's events that fade and lose their significance as soon as the newspaper is recycled, but it is part of the age-old process of narrative and story that connects people of all times and all places to their environments and to each other.

As Forster (1927) has observed, all of us are Scheherazade's husband from the "Arabian Nights" in our desire to know what will happen next. The story is a primitive form that reaches back before writing to the origins of literature. Story has informed and taught as much as it has entertained and amused. Many newspapers in the late 1800s all but abandoned the traditional story as part of their content, but they could not remove its elements. As long as humans collaborate in creating the symbols of their existence, spinning webs of significance (Geertz, 1973) that constitute culture, they will tell stories and want to know what happens next. Mass media have become the most prominent arenas for these activities, and while it is likely that the forms of delivery, transmission, and sharing of information and news will change dramatically, it is not likely that people will need story and narrative any less.

The public may need them much more. Media proliferate with hundreds of television channels, and cable and satellite networks; specialized magazines; thousands of newsletters; low-power radio and television stations; newspapers and newspaper bulletin boards; data banks on computer; computer data services, videotext and alternatives; interactive services involving the telephone, computer, and television set; virtual reality scenarios; and whatever else is in the technological pipeline. Just the traditional media people attend daily, coupled with mail, billboards and other advertisements, personal contacts, and pamphlets, leaflets, and fliers, offer far more facts than any of us can assimilate. Often, the daily accumulation of information provides little or no context. Our argument for narrative and story as means of bringing people together, and thereby building community, will be considered ironic by those familiar with some theorists, including Cooley (1925), who suggested that the shift toward fact and objectivity in the early 1800s was a move to create community. The argument, essentially, was that America was a fragmenting, if not fragmented, society, and that fact and objectivity in news would provide a common ground—a foundation on which to build participation in a common discourse. Objectivity and fact would build community, or at least compensate for the loss of traditional community structures.

Despite a century or so of supposedly objective, fact-oriented journalism, many of us still decry the loss of community or its changing nature. It may be that this is a nostalgic utopianism, with little meaning for our society at the millennium. Still, we find it impossible to dismiss the notion that human beings are social creatures who find knowledge, comfort, and safety in communication and community. Facts are necessary for us to learn and grow, but today's explosion of facts and information cannot by itself provide us with common elements on which to build community discourse. Narrative and story, in part because they provide context and linkage, are more conducive to human interaction and, therefore, to human community.

Given the array of fragmented, decontextualized information now available to people, it should be no surprise that some newspapers are rediscovering story forms. In a world that bombards people with information and facts—and with information posing as fact—story and narrative can be comforting and even reassuring. A narrative piece offers more context, and, potentially, more accessibility than a straight reporting of facts. It is an *accounting for*, not just an *accounting of*, the facts. It is surely more inviting, not only to read, but also to be part of. Audiences do not "receive" stories from without as much as they read and hear from within the story form. A redefinition from receiver to participant parallels our hope that news "consumers" somehow may be rejuvenated as a democratic "public." Narrative and story well done make the world more understandable, in the sense that it can be better understood, than the aggregation of facts.

Story is a creation, but so is—if we are honest—any journalism. The world's events do not happen in any journalistic form; they are molded by reporters and writers as they discover, create, or make the news. Each of us, whether or not we write news, makes up stories about the world around us. It is a natural activity. Even when we have only a few scattered facts or bits of information, our tendency is to attempt to give them significance through some kind of story. Narrative and story bring readers closer to events and people involved in them, and closer to the paper and reporters responsible for writing about them. All are involved in the story, which is part of the conversation of news, not its definitive explication. Conversation, in this sense, is a fruitful metaphor for news historians and other researchers. Rich in resonance, connections, and parallels, it allows us to see news beyond its most limited definition as fresh facts and a narrow interpretation of its surveillance function.

The metaphor holds for journalists themselves. Reporters cannot be "historians of the present" because they lack the advantage of looking back. The reporter and the historian create different worlds. The reporter has the advantage of living the present; seeing, feeling, touching and tasting news episodes; being part of events with their drama, pageantry, or even mundane dullness. While historians can *view* persons and their contributions, journalists can *interview* them. This is both an advantage and a disadvantage. After all, the historian has the advantage of living the past; poring through not only interviews for public consumption, but diaries, journals, snippets of recorded conversations, other people's reactions and comments; reconstructing the event and imagining what it looked and felt like; being part of the event from perspectives of not only many people, but of time.

Time and all the preceding, succeeding, and concurrent events, trends, and interpretations make the historian's perspective far different and more complete—and certainly more complex—than the reporter's. Neither perspective is necessarily the Truth. Both are constructed out of the materials at hand and both are parts of larger, perhaps more coherent conversations. While reporters cannot be historians, they can adopt more of the historian's concern for context. Reporters can add perspective and interpretation; they can certainly supplement the traditional journalistic form.

The artificial split between "news" and "story" resulted in the fragmentation of both news and newsworkers. Journalism came to think in terms of "news" and "entertainment," as though the two were mutually exclusive and to think in terms of "reporting" and "writing" as though the two were necessarily independent—the serious "reporter" and the entertaining "writer." In recent years some news outlets somewhat altered these roles. The recession scare of the late 1980s and early 1990s forced newspapers to rethink content and presentation, and one result has been a loosening up of forms. "Narrative" became a journalistic buzzword, but it should be more than that.

Story is powerful; it is an attitude as well as a form. It is not a quick fix but a commitment. While many journalists are quite capable of telling the news in story or narrative form, many simply are not. It is not necessarily that they lack writing skills, but they lack much of what it takes to get to the point of writing. It is not even reporting, though that may be part of it. They lack the whole attitude of approaching people, not just as sources, but as coequals or partners in a story. The approach of journalism has been that journalists are the keepers of truth, and certainly its discoverers. They know where it is, they find it, and they decide which portions of it to write and print. Sources certainly can manipulate, as any Washington (and most political) reporters will tell you, but the overall exchange is from reporter to reader in a transmission, relaying, delivering, and laying down of information, knowledge, and truth.

News as story forces writers and readers to see beyond straight facts; it forces information into some kind of context and it requires a broader vision and understanding. It need not be less accurate. Seeing news as stories in a conversation does not invest each item with undue importance; rather, it implies that each article is part of something bigger and, ultimately, more coherent. Each article may not be the final Truth, but it is part of the conversation in which people work toward truths and attempt to construct their own realities as they make sense out of the world and themselves.

8

Journalism's Emerging Agenda: Toward a Journalism that Communicates

For journalism to address the challenges of a conversation-based model, changes must come in how it is taught and practiced. We focus our agenda on journalism education, where techniques, attitudes, and conventions are reinforced, much of the labor pool is replenished, and many of journalism's most prominent spokespersons reside. Journalism education is not now in desperate straits and should retain and buttress much of the curriculum and classroom experience of college journalism majors. Many of its goals are laudable and must be retained and even reinforced. Few other programs on campuses offer such a unique blend of practical and intellectual learning, along with near-total immersion in the impact of the written word and direct experience with everyday social events. Where some other majors might depend on hypothetical cases, lectures, and professors' advice, journalism departments typically go beyond these devices to ask students to meet learning head-on by talking with people in the community and by reporting, explaining, and interpreting events and issues. The experiential emphasis of a strong, balanced journalism program produces students who are among a university's most liberally educated. Unfortunately, however, all is not well.

We suggest a serious discussion of several changes. Despite their strengths, journalism departments and schools can ill afford to be walled fiefdoms isolated from surrounding disciplines. Some elitism has characterized journalism, which, ironically, is essentially a populist profession. Other disciplines, naturally, may be just as elitist, but journalism is least able to absorb the costs of arrogance. Graduates from journalism programs become the sensory scouts of the mediated society—the eyes, ears, and consciousness, if not always the conscience, of social life. How can we maintain breadth in the issues of journalism education while diminishing some of its disciplinary insularity and preparing graduates to enter the social conversation as speakers and listeners, not just reporters?

Agenda Item 1: Journalism must be taught as one concentration in a network of complementary communication disciplines, not as an isolated profession with separate skills, ground rules, and structure. We believe this motion has three implications. First it suggests some adjustment of the metaphors commonly used in journalism education. Professors and textbooks customarily talk of the journalist's responsibility in order to "cover" (as with a blanket) events, beats, or "sources" in order to "uncover" (as in "dig up") facts, which can then be "reported" objectively to the public. Schudson (1978a) accurately predicted more than a decade ago that "what is likely to happen in schools of journalism and in newsrooms around the country as new recruits enter the field is that they will be told to forget the romance of newspaper work and to learn the same old basics of who, what, where, when reporting. They will be encouraged to reenact the rituals of objective reporting" (p. 192).

If exposed to this disciplinary rhetoric often enough, students begin to accept it: facts are out there; all you have to do is dig for them so that they might be presented unvarnished to a public who will apply them toward rational decisions. No wonder there is a trace of elitism now and then in "J students." The flaw in the picture is that such rhetoric conflicts with virtually all communication research in other social science disciplines. Communication is no longer researched or conceptualized as an objective sequence of transporting information, but rather is now seen as a complex process of persons negotiating relationships, often in the midst of unacknowledged subjectivity, prejudice, and incomplete understanding of intentions. However, journalism students typically are not required or encouraged to take courses in mainstream communication theory.

Instead of basic reliance on the "reporting" and "coverage" metaphors of a one-way delivery of information, educators can supplement and enhance education with interactive metaphors. Of course, reporting remains a central aspect of the job; but "negotiating," "sensitizing," and "facilitating," for example, are aspects as well. We miss too much when we study social patterns as if they issue directly from media messages. The *conversational* theme encourages exploration into the interaction "between the audience member and the media rather than a narrowly defined 'effect' of media on the audience" (Neumann, Just, & Crigler, 1992, p. 17). "This [constructionist] model of communication as 'conversation' provides a particularly attractive model for mass communications researchers" because it emphasizes the communicators' "implicit negotiations" of meaning (p. 17).

Second, a constructionist model encourages journalism's academic practitioners to see the profession as itself being newsworthy in the intellectual sphere. Although extremely bright men and women enter journalism and journalism education, many of them (with some notable exceptions) define the field so exclusively as a "professional-technical" endeavor that they exempt themselves from intellectual discussion and debate. This is why Janet Malcolm's (1990) accusations concerning the profession's inherently manipulative relationship with its subjects and its presumed flexibility in quoting interviewees not only created a furor for their venom but also *made news* (Anderson & Killenberg, 1992; Killenberg & Anderson, 1993). Such intellectual controversies, which can range over the landscape of ideas in communication, law, literary theory, and psychoanalysis, are too rare. Journalists who otherwise would not stomach the substance of Malcolm's accusations actually applauded her for shaking things up within this usually staid club. A newsworthy journalism is one fascinated by a full participation in communication research and speculation; to survive, it must attract students who are excited by ideas at least as much as by careers.

Third, journalism students must learn, more than they typically do in their programs, about the dynamics of interpersonal, face-to-face talk. Disciplinary turf protection is at stake here (or perhaps many experienced journalists have already developed impressive interpersonal skills on their own and believe that students similarly should learn them in practice). Alternatively, it may be that journalism professors are unaware of the increasing sophistication with which interpersonal communication researchers and teachers can help journalistic interviewers solve their applied communication problems. Students deserve better than to be limited by antiintellectual and self-defeating attitudes that result in the derision of research into nonverbal or interpersonal communication. The new generation of journalists, who are challenged to communicate sensitively across differences of race, gender, and class, are well advised to avoid such parochialism. Nonetheless, we fear that many influential and otherwise effective teachers leave such stigmata on the attitudes of young, developing journalists.

What, specifically, do journalists need to understand in the interpersonal sphere? The problems imposed on the journalist by the interview process cannot be underestimated. Interviews, quite apart from the mythology of neutral objectivity that the profession encourages, are occasions in which journalists inevitably and profoundly influence outcomes by their prior reputations, choices of situational context, questioning styles, nonverbal and verbal reactions, methods of recording, and—above all—listening styles. It is not so much what interviewees know, or even are willing to say, that is important; it is that interviewees make speech decisions in the context of particular interviewers and particular social situations. No matter who one "knows," no one is "ready to talk" independent of such personal questions as, "Who am I talking with?" "Will she give me a fair shake?" "Is he still listening?" "Does she understand my culture?"

Teaching tomorrow's journalists without reminding them constantly about the complications of dialogue impoverishes the profession not only conceptually but pragmatically. The need for increased interpersonal sensitivity in journalism introduces another related concern—that of cross-cultural sensitivity.

Agenda Item 2: Journalism should be taught as the public forum and arena for multicultural dialogue in a democracy. Multicultural education is not a fad. Hula hoops, skirt lengths, frisbees, and Batman may come and go, but majority and minority cultures have always been challenged to work together in an industrialized society that cannot afford human throwaways. American education has finally realized that diversity, properly invited and accepted, is invigorating rather than draining. It energizes the majority culture and creates cultural spaces and clearings in which minority cultures potentially can thrive and find identity without becoming exploited. We cannot now retreat from this commitment.

A commitment to diversity, however, requires an open journalism, accessible to all cultural groups. By "open journalism," we do not mean simply a free press unfettered by government control or censorship, but rather one that is equally accessible to all cultural groups. We argue further for an openness by individual journalists and news organizations to the nuances of talk and behavior that characterize racial, ethnic, and life-style groups of a pluralistic culture and informed tolerance for those styles that are most divergent from journalists' own. Even beyond these levels of openness, we propose that journalism structure communication contexts and opportunities so that diverse groups might begin to talk and listen *across their differences* to create a semblance of common knowledge about common problems. Educators must not shirk from teaching journalism as a *public philosophy*.

To teach journalism in higher education inevitably is to take a stand concerning political philosophy. We either ignore the complex relationship of public dialogue, opinion, and policy in our teaching (thereby implying that journalism is a technical task of communicating information accurately) or we reconceptualize journalism education as a multicultural process of negotiating political realities. Either way, journalism is taking a position regarding a political philosophy. As the posters from the 1960s used to say, "Not to decide is to decide."

Agenda Item 3: News organizations—academic or professional—should strive to start more conversations than they stop or settle. Media historian John Pauly (1990) put our concern for conversational process in perspective when examining journalism's take on "truth":

> The strongest objection to conventional journalism's truth is not that it claims to be representational or objective, but that it unilaterally asserts rather than fully argues its truth claims. The strength of a newspaper's interpretations are rarely tested by a community of readers. Because the daily newspaper carries an astonishing number and variety of stories each day, single stories escape the scrutiny that has been directed toward many New Journalism stories. Individual readers have neither the time nor the knowledge to verify the truthfulness of all the stories each day, nor are the newspaper's consumer-readers organized into a stable oppositional community that could provide the psychic, informational, or financial resources to dispute the accounts of large news organizations. (p. 122)

News accounts are presented as the truth as ascertained on that day, and either taken as such by their audiences or perhaps dismissed without sufficient warrant. If journalism's tendency is to assert rather than to argue its positions, then responsible reactions and subsequent dialogue are stifled. Journalism's claims, when taken as commodities or ammunition, are ill-suited to an ongoing conversation of positions.

David Zarefsky (1992) did not blame the media for what he perceives as our rhetorically impoverished public sphere. Instead, he identified two deeper causes: "first, that we depend on news media to play a far greater educational role than they are able to perform, and second, that we have allowed ourselves to conceive of our political system in media terms. We have fashioned a 'postmodern public' which has the trappings *but not the substance* of life in the *polis*" (p. 414, emphasis in original). Zarefsky concluded his essay: "Instead of cultivating argument, we have truncated the public space, distanced people from politics, emptied 'the public' of meaning as a collective noun, and trivialized such means for citizens' expression as responding to public opinion polls, calling '900' numbers, or showing up to cast a ballot on Election Day. Rather than praise or blame the media for our plight, we would be better advised to focus on the larger issue of how to revitalize the public sphere" (p. 414). Zarefsky is right not to brand the news media as scapegoats, but as we approach comparable problems of diminished discourse from a somewhat different angle, we sense that he may have overlooked a valid role for journalism in the revival that he and others seek.

Journalism can be a potent community-reminding, if not community-building, force. Yet its potential has never been fully encouraged in this regard, probably because we have been too busy selling to ourselves and our students a commodity model of news and straining toward more efficient and objective reporting techniques. Assuming a central place in a community of differences becomes a tall order for journalism and invites ridicule from naysayers for being an unrealistic, perhaps arrogant role. However, we should not bridle our goals too readily to an artificially limited vision. Let us ask the question: "If not here, where?" Where else should a society look for institutional access and assistance in communicating across differences: a cynical politics of campaigning, lobbying, and partisan appointments, Wall Street and corporate mega-interests, or the church in an era of tenuous affiliation? Journalism may well be the only community game in town, or at least the best playing field; our society will encounter more serious trouble if journalists elect not to play.

The most direct way in which journalism now attempts to sponsor a community-building forum is by conducting and reporting the results of public opinion polls as if the numbers were themselves commodities of hard news. At best, citizens learn to use poll trends to transform (or bolster) their personal value systems by positioning their own ideas relative to others. In this way, some basic requirements of democratic participation are satisfied, and at least what Boorstin (1970) once called "consumption communities"—an amorphous collage of brand loyalties, Reebok mania, and identification with mineral waters—might be acknowledged. We create new problems, however, when we rely almost exclusively on polling as our avenue to understanding what has come to be termed public opinion and what we can learn from it. Lippmann's (1922) skepticism about the inevitable idiosyncrasy and distortion of private opinions is only the cold, suspicious tip of this iceberg. More recently we have seen that in much polling, the act of asking plants the answer; that is, people often do not form attitudes about social issues until asked about them. In the process of answering, they invent in the moment whatever content subsequently gets reported. We know, too, through Noelle-Neumann's research (1984), that people inwardly monitor what they consider to be socially prevailing beliefs and attitudes in others and become reluctant to express discrepant views. The resulting *spiral of silence* in a publicly mediated democracy means that minority opinions on many issues may be expressed less often than they are held, which therefore makes other persons of the same persuasion even less likely to express their views and the majority more likely to assert theirs. The minority status of some social attitudes becomes, therefore, perpetually frozen, incapable of attracting support because of, not in spite of, the workings of a "free press."

Increasingly, such socially suspect data is being tied not only to innocent issues of popularity but to serious issues of policy. Contemporary politicians are tempted to decide policies based on polling data rather than on the merits of alternatives. Here is a new twist on rationality; although this preoccupation with public perception is not new, it is newly effective, from the politician's perspective, in determining his or her individual success. The media ability to help a politician constantly monitor fluctuating personal popularity might irrevocably deflect governmental policy debate from issue-based and ethical questions of "What should we do?" to the image-based question, "How are we doing in the polls?" Insider leaks and trial balloons become ploys in such a gaming strategy: "We'll test the waters with an 'unnamed source' leak—then if public reaction isn't positive, we'll disavow it." Some persuasive evidence now shows why this ominous projection in fact becomes rational behavior for the political actor. "With the Bush presidency," Fishkin (1991) wrote, "we have reached the point where a secretary of state, when questioned about the merits of his foreign policy, cites favorable poll results. Some have even charged that President Bush only began to emphasize the supposedly 'new urgency' of a possible Iraqi nuclear threat after poll results . . . showed that this danger was far more effective in justifying American intervention in the Persian Gulf than any other argument" (p. 47).

We can expect this trend of "poll-itics as usual" to continue as long as journalism maintains its conduit, reportorial tone and its individualistic emphases. Supplying individual readers and listeners with individual facts, however objectively, and then asking those individuals what they think is fine as far as it goes, but it necessarily depends on journalism as the major *subjective* player in both the input to and output of the system. Soliciting individual opinion and then aggregating the data implies that a "public" is equal to the sum of its collective attitudes. A recent *Newsweek* cover story (Fineman, 1993) on the impact of talk-show politics in Campaign '92 made this same point. A public is not the sum of its individual attitudes any more than a class is the sum of its ACT scores.

In contrast, Fishkin (1991) and other political philosophers have suggested that aggregated individual opinion, which is usually based on misinformation, disinformation, or outright ignorance, is not at all the same as "public opinion" and is far from the result we would get if we could sample what people's ideas would be if they had the opportunity to discuss issues with other representative and informed citizens. Fishkin recommends a "national caucus" plan that would provide a "deliberative opinion poll" facilitated by media coverage and dramatization. This approach, he argues, would avoid the modeling of what the electorate *does think* in an inadequate information environment, as now, and instead would provide a model for what a statistically constructed sample of interacting people can tell us and *would think* if afforded adequate information and an opportunity for dialogue with other persons of diverse opinions. Fishkin's suggestion addresses democratic ills conversationally, but on a grand scale. Short of implementing a massive national caucus program, though, journalism might more widely adopt the same fundamental principles and reminders to elevate political and cultural dialogue in contemporary society.

Agenda Item 4: Journalism education must more clearly delineate for students the ethical and moral contexts of the field. Ethics is often a part of journalism programs, and instructors usually discuss reporting in terms of ethical choices. The classroom focus, however, is almost always on the behavior of the journalist. This orientation—the "What do I do now?" approach— is better than no discussion of ethical choice points at all, but it encourages the journalist to see the nexus of ethics as his or her own personal possession and invites a trouble-shooting or crisis-management ethical model at best. Although individual journalists encounter concrete, immediate problems and should anticipate them, a narrow, personal preoccupation with such a perspective can cloud or entirely displace another equally crucial aspect of journalistic ethics—a consideration of the broader ethical context for public life. "What do I do now?" ethical approaches stress a deontic, principle-based logic. Explicitly or implicitly, students are told that journalism holds some standards so dear ("unbiased truth" or "objectivity," confidentiality of sources, separation of news and editorial functions, etc.) that its practitioners are duty-bound to follow them with rare exception.

David Eason (1986), in analyzing the aftermath of the controversy over the Janet Cooke fabrication, argued that the journalistic community responded almost with a single voice in demonizing Cooke and condemning the betrayal of trust involved in her invention of "Jimmy," a supposedly real eight-year-old heroin addict in a story that won her a Pulitzer Prize in 1981. The outrage was a symbolic reaffirmation of journalism's "oneness in disapproving of Cooke's violation" (p. 430). "The picture that emerges from much of the writing on Janet Cooke is of a unified community of journalists betrayed" by Cooke (pp. 433–434), since she so obviously violated the principle of truth. A ritual symbolic cleansing after the affair sought to restore journalistic credibility through expulsion of the offender, removal of her prize, and reaffirmation of the simple principle of honest portrayal in journalism. However, as Eason showed, the journalistic line between fact and fiction had become too blurred for such repair efforts to be persuasive to a public already confused by what kinds of authority to grant journalism in the first place.

The familiar classroom discussion of the various professional codes is further testimony to the normative tradition of journalistic ethics. We hope that instructors will invite students to critique such principles or duties, in addition to remembering them, and also to critique how they might be applied in given cases.

Deontological reasoning in ethics sounds better in the classroom or in a managing editor's conference than it does on the streets. This is not news to working reporters, of course, but it may help to explain why some groups—social, ethnic, cultural, sexual preference, economic—might engage in behaviors that would violate typical journalistic principles yet might also be seen as "ethical" from within the group's differing set of assumptions. Janet Cooke's transgression was clearly unacceptable in terms of the usual expectations for credible journalism. However, the profession's tendency to condemn Cooke with "one voice" might indicate the extent to which a standard-based ethic (which was implemented) might be supplemented with a more contextual, relational ethic (which was not). Although Cooke's race (African-American) was widely discussed, it tended to be discussed in terms of how journalistic standards might have been lowered in some cases to encourage minority reporters. Moreover, the possible relevance of Cooke's gender was barely discussed (Eason, 1986, p. 434). No defense of Cooke is implied here; we merely suggest that a wider lens might have been employed to contextualize ethical choices within society.

The potential for wide journalistic dialogue (beyond condemnation) about the implications of the Cooke incident was lost. Any debate about Cooke's specific behavior would surely be brief (she did lie about her story, after all); however, the field of journalism neglected to explore several other important issues of ethical breadth. Could journalism itself, saturated in larger social trends, have been encouraging its practitioners to blur the lines between fact and fiction to tell a fuller story? Could African-American journalists experience special pressures to try to get inner-city traumas told with impact in white-controlled major-city papers? Could minority journalists occasionally be more resonant to street ethics? Might many women journalists experience ethical dilemmas on somewhat different and less deontic grounds? Does a journalist's involvement with a narrative approach imply a somewhat different ethical slant? Journalists need to consider not only what their own ethical standards and choices might be; they also need to be able to explain the broader contextual climate in which *other* choices might be justified.

One prominent and often controversial issue is particularly challenging for journalism ethics. The traditionally male orientation of journalism has probably left its mark on the kinds of ethical discussion deemed appropriate in classrooms and later in newsrooms. The work in ethics and moral reasoning done by Noddings (1984), Gilligan (1982), Belenky and colleagues (1986), Benhabib (1992), and others indicates that men and women in Western industrialized society tend to frame ethical issues differently. Women, the research suggests, tend to base ethical decision making less on principle than on relationship, less on isolated "facts" and more on a holistic estimate of emotional context, and less on rational proofs than on narrative evidence. Whereas men tend to discuss ethics more in terms of what to say and do (the traditionally journalistic approach), women tend to approach moral problems from the vantage points of listening, empathizing, caring, and creating a context of explanation in which behavior might be more meaningfully understood (Noddings, 1984; Tannen, 1990). If this is true, the very basis for Western journalistic ethics can be seen as decidedly uncongenial to many women and their communication decisions. If true, it is also small wonder that men are so ready to reach decisive news conclusions when they think they have the facts while women are often less sure of the weight of fact in a given case and may want to talk more with the people involved in order to get the feel of a situation. Small wonder, too, that women usually keep the concept of relationship rather than that of intransigent principle in the forefront of their moral reasoning.

While we are not urging an institutional feminization of news, any profession needs a balance of principle and contextual exception, a balance between allegiance to duty and allegiance to relationship. The dualism is ultimately artificial; both perspectives, along with diverse positions between them, are necessary. Our estimate of their relation is one of proportion rather than competition. Duty to principle and concern for human relationship are not at odds, although a consideration of them simultaneously can certainly lead to a creative tension that will ultimately improve journalistic practice.

Journalism has privileged the male voice, and the effects are wider than just the outcomes of who joins the profession or which stories are emphasized. The male voice has affected the very definition of ethical choice in the field. Journalism, in effect, has—without plotting to do so—institutionalized a masculine notion of the single ethical answer, the desirability of the "clearcut" standard. This does not mean there are no arguments about what that standard ought to be in a given instance. Rather, this recognition reminds us that the criterion of a duty-based "standard" is rarely questioned. We should not be lulled into thinking we can dismiss, trivialize, or, from some pedestal, criticize broader cultural ambiguities in ethics. A wider foundation must be poured for multigroup sensitivities in ethics, and the proper site to begin these discussions is the journalism program in higher education.

Agenda Item 5: News organizations must stress narrative knowing more prominently to supplement scientific knowing. Throughout *The Conversation of Journalism* we have supported the news functions of reporting, but not as the sole focus for the field. As some observers (Lasch, 1990) have noted, the elevation of fact-based reportage and objectivity neatly coincided with the rise of industrial technology and the increasingly pervasive scientific and positivist tenor in the West. Ironically, to Lasch, public debate "began to decline . . . when the press became more 'responsible,' more professional, more conscious of its civic obligations" (p. 17).

The definition of news changed along with our definition for what kind of society we thought we could have—it was now defined as efficient, predictable, orderly, and objectively reported-on and governed. To the extent that society became increasingly mechanized and, people presumed, predictable, people demanded a news environment consistent with an increasingly efficiency-driven society. Lasch pointed out that government was more participatory in the nineteenth century when newspapers themselves participated in public controversies and discussed them in language "still shaped by the rhythms and requirements of the spoken word, in particular by the conventions of verbal argumentation. Print served to create a larger forum for the spoken word, not yet to displace or reshape it" (1990, p. 18). Later, news was to become objectified, in part because as a public, we believed that objective, scientific thinking was crucial to ordering our lives. In many ways, it was, but what was lost?

The history of early American journalism, in particular, discloses to contemporary readers many surprising examples of subjectively written indictments, authorial personalizations, and (by contemporary expectations) overdramatized accounts (Dardenne, 1990). Newspaper practices in the late nineteenth century were characterized by the tension between what Schudson (1978a, pp. 89 ff.) called "two journalisms," whereby the "ideal of the story" competed with the "ideal of information."

Today, "newstelling" as a conversational approach to news could help recover aspects of early journalism's community involvement, vigor, and sense of drama. Although some fear that narrative coherence and narrative fidelity are incompatible, newstelling can indeed engage people and address important issues yet, as we show in Chapter 7, still be consistent with fairness and clarity.

We hope that the conversation we describe and promote will continue to consider the issues raised in these pages. Our agenda remains open, as we ask you, as readers and citizens, to discuss and debate it, to add to and subtract from it. We offer it as part of the "unending conversation" described by Kenneth Burke (1957):

Where does the [social] drama get its material? From the 'unending conversation' that is going on at the point in history when we are born. Imagine that you enter a parlor. You come late. When you arrive, others have long preceded you, and they are engaged in a heated discussion, a discussion too heated for them to pause and tell you exactly what it is about. In fact, the discussion had already begun long before any of them got there, so that no one present is qualified to retrace for you all the steps that had gone before. You listen for a while, until you decide that you have caught the tenor of the argument; then you put in your oar. Someone answers; you answer him; another comes to your defense; another aligns himself against you, to either the embarrassment or gratification of your opponent, depending upon the quality of your ally's assistance. However, the discussion is interminable. The hour grows late, you must depart. And you do depart, with the discussion still vigorously in progress. (pp. 94–96)

A journalism elevating conversation is more interesting, inviting, powerful, inclusive, realistic, and, ultimately, more informative than a journalism that attempts to portray our lives as events, facts, and truths chronicled, day after day, in definitive articles. The public is part of a journalism that *talks with it*, *listens to it*, and *enables its own talk.* Conversation defines and shapes human life, and through conversation, we can learn about our world and participate in it. Journalism can add its voice and the voice of many others to that conversation, or it can stand apart, talking largely to itself in a monologue of questionable relevance, value, and purpose.

References

Anderson, R. (in press). Anonymity, presence, and the dialogic self in a technological culture. In R. Anderson, K. N. Cissna, & R. C. Arnett (Eds.), *The reach of dialogue: Confirmation, voice, and community*. Cresskill, NJ: Hampton Press.

Anderson, R., & Killenberg, G. M. (1985). Teaching students an ear for news. *Journalism Educator, 40*, 54–57.

Anderson, R., & Killenberg, G. M. (1992). Journalistic listening and "slanted empathy": Ethical implications of the Janet Malcolm accusations. *Journal of the International Listening Association, 6*, 66–82.

Asante, M. K. (1992). Multiculturalism: An exchange. In P. Berman (Ed.), *Debating P.C.* (pp. 299–311). New York: Dell.

Atkinson, P. (1990). *The ethnographic imagination: Textual constructions of reality*. London: Routledge.

Baggot, T. (1992, November/December). Personal involvement: Journalists, compassion, and the common good. *Quill*, pp. 26, 27.

Bakhtin, M. M. (1981). *The dialogic imagination: Four essays* (C. Emerson & M. Holquist, Trans.). Austin: University of Texas Press.

Bakhtin, M. M. (1986). *Speech genres and other late essays* (V. McGee, Trans.). Austin: University of Texas Press.

Banaszynski, J. (1988, April). AIDS in the heartland. *St. Paul Pioneer Press Dispatch* reprint, p. 1.

Belenky, M. F., Clinchy, B. M., Goldberger, N. R., & Tarule, J. M. (1986). *Women's ways of knowing: The development of self, voice, and mind.* New York: Basic Books.

Bellah, R. N., Madsen, R., Sullivan, W. M., Swidler, A., & Tipton, S. M. (1986). *Habits of the heart: Individualism and commitment in American life.* New York: Harper & Row.

Bellah, R. N., Madsen, R., Sullivan, W. M., Swidler, A., & Tipton, S. M. (1991). *The good society.* New York: Random House.

Benhabib, S. (1992). *Situating the self: Gender, community, and postmodernism in contemporary ethics.* New York: Routledge.

Bennett, W. L. (1988). *News: The politics of illusion.* New York: Longman.

Berger, P., Berger, B., & Kellner, H. (1974). *The homeless mind: Modernization and consciousness.* New York: Vintage Books.

Berger, P., & Luckmann, T. (1966). *The social construction of reality: A treatise in the sociology of knowledge.* New York: Doubleday.

Biagi, S. (1992). *Interviews that work: A practical guide for journalists* (2nd ed.). Belmont, CA: Wadsworth.

Bird, S. E. (1992). *For enquiring minds: A cultural study of supermarket tabloids.* Knoxville: University of Tennessee Press.

Bird, S. E., & Dardenne, R. W. (1988). Myth, chronicle, and story: Exploring the narrative qualities of news. In J. W. Carey (Ed.), *Media, myths and narratives: Television and the press* (pp. 67–86). Newbury Park, CA: Sage.

Bird, S. E., & Dardenne, R. W. (1990). News and storytelling in American culture: Reevaluating the sensational dimension. *Journal of American Culture, 13,* 33–38.

Bohm, D. (1985). *Unfolding meaning: A weekend of dialogue with David Bohm.* London: Ark.

Boorstin, D. (1961). *The image.* New York: Atheneum.

Boorstin, D. (1970). *The decline of radicalism: Reflections on America today.* New York: Vintage.

Booth, W. C. (1974). *Modern dogma and the rhetoric of assent.* Chicago: University of Chicago Press.

Booth, W. C. (1988). *The vocation of a teacher: Rhetorical occasions, 1967–1988.* Chicago: University of Chicago Press.

Boulding, K. (1971). *The image: Knowledge in life and society.* Ann Arbor, MI: Ann Arbor Paperback.

Breed, W. (1955). Social control in the newsroom. *Social Forces, 33,* 326–335.

Brown, R. H. (1987). *Society as text: Essays on rhetoric, reason, and reality.* Chicago: University of Chicago Press.

Bruner, J. (1986). *Actual minds, possible worlds.* Cambridge, MA: Harvard University Press.

Bruner, J. (1990). *Acts of meaning*. Cambridge, MA: Harvard University Press.

Buber, M. (1965). *The knowledge of man: A philosophy of the interhuman* (M. Friedman, Trans.). New York: Harper & Row.

Burke, K. (1957). *The philosophy of literary form*. New York: Vintage Books.

Burke, K. (1967). Rhetoric—Old and new. In M. Steinmann, Jr. (Ed.), *New rhetorics* (pp. 60–76). New York: Charles Scribner's Sons.

Burke, K. (1969). *A rhetoric of motives*. Berkeley: University of California Press.

Burke, P. (Ed.). (1991). *New perspectives on historical writing*. University Park: Pennsylvania State University Press.

Campbell, J. (1982). *Grammatical man: Information, entropy, language, and life*. New York: Simon and Schuster.

Carey, J. W. (1975). A cultural approach to communication. *Communication*, 2, 1–22.

Carey, J. W. (1986). The dark continent of American journalism. In R. K. Manoff & M. Schudson (Eds.), *Reading the news* (pp. 146–196). New York: Pantheon.

Carey, J. W. (1989). *Communication as culture: Essays on media and society*. Boston: Unwin Hyman.

Carey, J. W. (1991). "A republic, if you can keep it": Liberty and public life in the age of Glasnost. In R. Arsenault (Ed.), *Crucible of liberty: 200 years of the bill of rights* (pp. 108–128). New York: Free Press.

Carmondy, D. (1993, July 26). Time's readers to talk back, on computers. *New York Times*, p. C6.

Chomsky, N. (1989). *Necessary illusions*. Boston: South End Press.

Cissna, K. N., & Anderson, R. (in press). Communication and the ground of dialogue. In R. Anderson, K. N. Cissna, & R. C. Arnett (Eds.), *The reach of dialogue: Confirmation, voice, and community*. Cresskill, NJ: Hampton Press.

Cohan, S., & Shires, L. M. (1988). *Telling stories*. London: Routledge.

Cohen, S., & Young, J. (Eds). (1981). *The manufacture of news: Social problems, deviance and the mass media*. London: Constable.

Coles, R. (1989). *The call of stories: Teaching and the moral imagination*. Boston: Houghton Mifflin.

Cooley, C. H. (1925). *Social organization: A study of the larger mind*. New York: Charles Scribner's Sons.

Crapanzano, V. (1992). *Hermes' dilemma and Hamlet's desire: On the epistemology of interpretation*. Cambridge, MA: Harvard University Press.

Cronon, W. (1992, March). A place for stories: Nature, history, and narrative. *Journal of American History*, pp. 1347–1376.

Cunningham, R. P. (1993, January/February). Editor, once burned, finds new empathy for the misquoted. *Quill*, pp. 8, 9.

Czitrom, D. (1982). *Media and the American mind*. Chapel Hill: University of North Carolina Press.

Dardenne, R. (1990). *Newstelling: Story and themes in "The Courant" of Hartford from 1765 to 1945*. Unpublished doctoral dissertation, University of Iowa, Iowa City.

Darnton, R. (1975). Writing news and telling stories. *Daedalus, 104*, 175–194.

Denzin, N. K. (1992). *Symbolic interactionism and cultural studies: The politics of interpretation*. Oxford, UK: Blackwell.

DeVito, J. A. (1986). *The communication handbook: A dictionary*. New York: Harper & Row.

Dewey, J. (1916). *Democracy and education: An introduction to the philosophy of education*. New York: Free Press.

Dewey, J. (1927). *The public and its problems*. Denver, CO: Alan Swallow.

Dewey, J., & Bentley, A. F. (1949). *Knowing and the known*. Boston: Beacon Press.

Downing, J. (1980). *The media machine*. London: Pluto Press.

Duncan, H. D. (1962). *Communication and social order*. London: Oxford University Press.

Eason, D. L. (1981). Telling stories and making sense. *Journal of Popular Culture, 15*, 121–129.

Eason, D. L. (1984). The new journalism and the image-world: Two modes of organizing experience. *Critical Studies in Mass Communication, 1*, 51–65.

Eason, D. L. (1986). On journalistic authority: The Janet Cooke scandal. *Critical Studies in Mass Communication, 3*, 429–447.

Elbow, P. (1973). *Writing without teachers*. London: Oxford University Press.

Ellul, J. (1985). *The humiliation of the word* (J. M. Hanks, Trans.). Grand Rapids: MI: William B. Eerdmans.

Entman, R. M. (1989). *Democracy without citizens*. New York: Oxford University Press.

Epstein, E. J. (1974). *News from nowhere*. New York: Vintage Books.

Etzioni, A. (1993). *The spirit of community*. New York: Crown Publishers.

Faludi, S. (1991). *Backlash: The undeclared war against American women*. New York: Crown Publishers.

Farson, R. (1978). The technology of humanism. *Journal of Humanistic Psychology, 18*, 5–35.

Ferrarotti, F. (1988). *The end of conversation: The impact of mass media on modern society*. Westport, CT: Greenwood.

Fineman, H. (1993, February 8). The power of talk. *Newsweek*, pp. 24–28.

Fischer, D. (1970). *Historians' fallacies*. New York: Harper Torchbooks.

Fisher, W. R. (1985). The narrative paradigm: In the beginning. *Journal of Communication, 35*, 74–89.

Fisher, W. R. (1987). *Human communication as narration: Toward a philosophy of reason, value, and action.* Columbia: University of South Carolina Press.

Fishkin, J. S. (1991). *Democracy and deliberation.* New Haven, CT: Yale University Press.

Fishkin, J. S. (1992). *The dialogue of justice: Toward a reflective society.* New Haven, CT: Yale University Press.

Fishman, M. (1980). *Manufacturing the news.* Austin: University of Texas Press.

Forster, E. M. (1927). *Aspects of the novel.* New York: Harvest/Harcourt Brace Jovanovich.

Fowler, R., Hodge, B., Kress, G., & Trew, T. (1979). *Language and control.* London: Routledge & Kegan Paul.

Freire, P. (1970). *Pedagogy of the oppressed.* New York: Seabury.

French, T. (1991, May 12–21). South of heaven. *St. Petersburg Times.*

Friedman, M. (1974). *Touchstones of reality: Existential trust and the community of peace.* New York: Dutton.

Gadamer, H.-G. (1982). *Truth and method* (2nd ed.; G. Barden & J. Cumming, Trans.). New York: Crossroad.

Gadamer, H.-G. (1989). Text and interpretation. In D. P. Michelfelder & R. E. Palmer (Eds.), *Dialogue and deconstruction: The Gadamer-Derrida encounter* (pp. 21–51). Albany: State University of New York Press.

Gans, H. (1979). *Deciding what's news.* New York: Pantheon.

Geertz, C. (1973). *The interpretation of cultures.* New York: Basic Books.

Gerbner, G. (1974). Teacher image in mass culture: Symbolic functions of the "hidden curriculum." In David Olson (Ed.), *Media and symbols* (pp. 470–473). Chicago: University of Chicago Press.

Gerbner, G. (1977, June). Television: The new state religion? *Et Cetera*, pp. 145–150.

Gersh, D. (1992, October 10). Promulgating polarization. *Editor & Publisher*, pp. 30, 48.

Gilligan, C. (1982). *In a different voice: Psychological theory and women's development.* Cambridge, MA: Harvard University Press.

Glasgow University Media Group. (1976). *Bad news.* London: Routledge & Kegan Paul.

Glasgow University Media Group. (1980). *More bad news.* London: Routledge & Kegan Paul.

Goldstein, T. (Ed.). (1989). *Killing the messenger: 100 years of media criticism.* New York: Columbia University Press.

Goodall, N. (1972). *Ecumenical progress.* London: Oxford University Press.

Greenfield, M. (1992, November 9). A year of surprises. *Newsweek*, p. 88.

Greider, W. (1992). *Who will tell the people?* New York: Simon & Schuster.

Grossberg, L., Nelson, C., & Treichler, P. (Eds.). (1992). *Cultural studies*. New York: Routledge.

Habermas, J. (1975). *Legitimation crisis* (T. McCarthy, Trans.). Boston: Beacon Press.

Habermas, J. (1979). *Communication and the evolution of society* (T. McCarthy, Trans.). Boston: Beacon Press.

Habermas, J. (1992). *Autonomy and solidarity* (rev. ed.; P. Drews, Ed.). London: Verso.

Hall, S. (1975). Introduction. In A.C.H. Smith (Ed.), *Paper voices: The popular press and social change, 1935–1965* (pp. 1–24). London: Chatto & Windus.

Hall, S. (1977). Culture, the media and the "ideological" effect. In J. Curran, M. Gurevitch, & J. Woolacott (Eds.), *Mass communication and society* (pp. 315–348). London: Edward Arnold.

Hall, S. (1984). The narrative construction of reality: An interview with Stuart Hall. *Southern Review, 17*(1), 3–17.

Hall, S. (1989). Ideology and communication theory. In B. Dervin, L. Grossberg, B. J. O'Keefe, & E. Wartella (Eds.), *Rethinking communication: Vol. 1. Paradigm issues* (pp. 40–52). Newbury Park, CA: Sage Publications.

Hall, S., Critcher, C., Jefferson, T., Clark, J. & Roberts, B. (1981). The social production of news: Mugging in the media. In S. Cohen & J. Young (Eds.), *The manufacture of news: Social problems and deviance in the mass media* (pp. 335–367). London: Constable.

Hallin, D. C. (1992a). The passing of the "high modernism" of American journalism. *Journal of Communication, 42*, 14–25.

Hallin, D. C. (1992b). Sound bite news: Television coverage of elections, 1968–1988. *Journal of Communication, 42*, 5–24.

Hart, J. (1992, May 2). A manner of speaking. *Editor & Publisher*, pp. 26, 111.

Hartley, J. (1982). *Understanding news*. London: Methuen.

Herman, E. S. (1992). *Beyond hypocrisy: Decoding the news in an age of propaganda*. Boston: South End Press.

Holquist, M. (1990). *Dialogism: Bakhtin and his world*. London: Routledge.

Howell, D. (1988, April). Pulitzer prize the final chapter in a poignant story. *St. Paul Pioneer Press Dispatch* reprint, p. 21.

Hughes, H. (1968). *News and the human interest story*. New York: Greenwood Press.

Jacobs, J. (1961). *The death and life of great American cities*. New York: Vintage Books.

James, S. (1991, April 14). A gift abandoned. *St. Petersburg Times*, reprint.

Jensen, J. (1990). *Redeeming modernity: Contradictions in media criticism*. Newbury Park, CA: Sage.

Jensen, M. C. (1977). *The sorry state of news reporting and why it won't be changed.* Speech to New York State Publishers Association, Rochester, NY.

Katz, J. (1992, March 5). Rock, rap and movies bring you the news. *Rolling Stone*, pp. 33, 36, 37, 40, 78.

Kelly, M., & Dowd, M. (1992, January 17). The company he keeps. *New York Times*, pp. 20–27, 34, 36, 48, 50–52.

Kennedy, B. (1974). *Community journalism: A way of life.* Ames: Iowa State University Press.

Killenberg, G. M. (1968). *Richard H. Amberg and the St. Louis Globe-Democrat: Twelve years of community service.* Unpublished master's thesis, Southern Illinois University, Carbondale, IL.

Killenberg, G. M., & Anderson, R. (1976). Sources are persons: Teaching interviewing as dialogue. *Journalism Educator, 31*, 16–20.

Killenberg, G. M., & Anderson, R. (1989). *Before the story: Interviewing and communication skills for journalists.* New York: St. Martin's Press.

Killenberg, G. M., & Anderson, R. (1993). What is a "quote?": Practical, rhetorical, and ethical concerns for journalists. *Journal of Mass Media Ethics, 8*, 37–54.

Kuralt, C. (1985). *On the road.* New York: G. P. Putnam's Sons.

Lacan, J. (1981). The empty word and the full word. In A. Wilden (Ed.), *Speech and language in psychoanalysis* (A. Wilden, Trans.). Baltimore: Johns Hopkins University Press.

Lasch, C. (1990, September). The lost art of political argument. *Harper's*, pp. 17–22.

Leigh, R. D. (Ed.). (1974). *A free and responsible press. A general report on mass communication: Newspapers, radio, motion pictures, magazines, and books. By the commission on freedom of the press.* Chicago: University of Chicago Press.

Levi-Strauss, C. (1963). *Structural anthropology.* New York: Basic Books.

Lippmann, W. (1922). *Public opinion.* New York: Free Press.

Lord, A. (1960). *The singer of tales.* Cambridge, MA: Harvard University Press.

McCormick, J., & Smith, V. E. (1992, November 9). Can we get along? *Newsweek*, pp. 70–72.

McIntosh, P. (1992, January/February). White privilege. Wellesley College Center for Research on Women, pp. 33–35, 53.

MacIntyre, A. (1984). *After virtue: A study in moral theory* (2nd ed.). Notre Dame, IN: University of Notre Dame Press.

McManus, J. H. (1992). What kind of commodity is news? *Communication Research, 19*, 787–805.

Malcolm, J. (1990). *The journalist and the murderer.* New York: Vintage Books.

Maranhao, T. (1990). *The interpretation of dialogue*. Chicago: University of Chicago Press.

Marzolf, M. T. (1991). *Civilizing voices: American press criticism 1880–1950*. New York: Longman.

Mead, G. H. (1925–1926). The nature of aesthetic experience. *International Journal of Ethics, 36*, 382–393.

Mead, G. H. (1934). *Mind, self and society: From the standpoint of a social behaviorist*. Chicago: University of Chicago Press.

Mead, G. H. (1956). *The social psychology of George Herbert Mead*. Chicago: University of Chicago Press.

Merrill, J. (1977). *Existential journalism*. New York: Hastings House.

Meyrowitz, J. (1985). *No sense of place: The impact of electronic media on social behavior*. New York: Oxford University Press.

Mindich, D.T.Z. (1993, August). Edwin M. Stanton, the inverted pyramid, and information control. *Journalism Monographs, 140*.

Molotch, H., & Lester, M. (1974). News as purposive behavior: On the strategic use of routine, events, accidents, and scandals. *American Sociological Review, 39*, 101–112.

Morrow, L. (1991, August 26). The provocative professor. *Time*, pp. 19, 20.

Mossberg, W. S. (1993, July 22). For now, the way to electronic papers goes through San Jose. *Wall Street Journal*, p. B1.

Moyers, B. (1971). *Listening to America*. New York: Harper & Row.

Moyers, B. (1989). *A world of ideas*. New York: Doubleday.

Moyers, B. (1992, March 29). For democracy's sake, we must recapture the mind of America. *St. Petersburg Times*, pp. 1D, 5D.

Munz, P. (1977). *The shapes of time*. Middletown, CT: Wesleyan University Press.

Murray, D. M. (1983). *Writing for your readers*. Chester, CT: Globe Pequot Press.

Murray, D. M. (1988, January). *Empathetic reporting* (Report No. 3). Boston: Boston Globe Writing on Writing Series.

National Advisory Commission on Civil Disorders. (1968). *Report of the National Advisory Commission on Civil Disorders*. New York: E. P. Dutton.

Neumann, W. R., Just, M. R., & Crigler, A. N. (1992). *Common knowledge: News and the construction of political meaning*. Chicago: University of Chicago Press.

Nisbet, R. A. (1966). *Sociological tradition*. New York: Basic Books.

Nisbet, R. A. (1973). *The social philosophers: Community and conflict in Western thought*. New York: Thomas Y. Crowell.

Nisbet, R. A. (1990). *The quest for community*. San Francisco: Institute for Contemporary Studies.

Noddings, N. (1984). *Caring: A feminine approach to ethics and moral education.* Berkeley: University of California Press.

Noelle-Neumann, E. (1984). *The spiral of silence: Public opinion—Our social skin.* Chicago: University of Chicago Press.

Nofsinger, R. E. (1991). *Everyday conversation.* Newbury Park, CA: Sage.

Oakeshott, M. (1959). *The voice of poetry in the conversation of mankind: An essay.* London: Bowes & Bowes.

Overholser, G. (1991, Spring). Making voters believers. *Nieman Reports,* pp. 22, 23, 38.

Park, R. (1944). News as a form of knowledge. *American Journal of Sociology, 45,* 669–686.

Park, R. (1955). *Society: collective behavior, news and opinion, sociology and modern society.* Glencoe, IL: Free Press.

Pauly, J. (1990). The politics of the new journalism. In N. Sims (Ed.), *Literary journalism in the twentieth century* (pp. 110–129). New York: Oxford University Press.

Peterman, P. (1992, May 26). A tree stands alone. *St. Petersburg Times,* pp. 1D, 2D.

Phillips, E. B. (1976). Novelty without change. *Journal of Communication, 27,* 17–92.

Postman, N. (1985). *Amusing ourselves to death.* New York: Penguin Books.

Rachlin, A. (1988). *News as hegemonic reality: American political culture and the framing of news accounts.* Westport, CT: Praeger.

Rafaeli, S. (1988). Interactivity: From new media to communication. In Hawkins, R. P., Wiemann, J. M., & Pingree, S. (Eds.), *Advancing communication science: Merging mass and interpersonal processes* (pp. 110–134). Newbury Park, CA: Sage.

Ransome, A. (1909). *The history of storytelling.* London: Jack.

Reid, L. (1978). *Hurry home Wednesday: Growing up in a small Missouri town, 1905–1921.* Columbia: University of Missouri Press.

Rice, R. E., & Associates. (1984). *The new media: Communication, research, and technology.* Beverly Hills, CA: Sage.

Richter, R. (1978). *Whose news? Politics, the press and the third world.* London: Burnett Books.

Ricoeur, P. (1980). Narrative time. In W.J.T. Mitchell (Ed.), *On narrative* (pp. 165–186). Chicago: University of Chicago Press.

Ridder, P. (1980, November/December). There are TK fact-checkers in the U.S. *Columbia Journalism Review,* p. 62.

Rock, P. (1981). News as eternal recurrence. In S. Cohen & J. Young (Eds.), *The manufacture of news: Social problems and deviance in the mass media* (pp. 64–70). London: Constable.

Romano, C. (1987). The grisly truth about bare facts. In R. K. Manoff & M. Schudson (Eds.), *Reading the news* (pp. 38–78). New York: Pantheon.

Rommetveit, R. (1987). Meaning, context, and control: Convergent trends and controversial issues in current social-scientific research on human cognition and communication. *Inquiry, 30*, 77–99.

Rorty, R. (1979). *Philosophy and the mirror of nature*. Princeton, NJ: Princeton University Press.

Rosen, J. (1991a). Making journalism more public. *Communication, 12*, 267–284.

Rosen, J. (1991b, October). To be or not to be. *ASNE Bulletin*, pp. 16–19.

Rosen, J., & Taylor, P. (1992). *The new news v. the old news*. New York: Twentieth Century Fund Press.

Roshco, B. (1975). *Newsmaking*. Chicago: University of Chicago Press.

Schama, S. (1991). *Dead certainties (unwarranted speculations)*. New York: Alfred A. Knopf.

Schiller, D. (1981). *Objectivity: The public and the rise of commercial journalism*. Philadelphia: University of Pennsylvania Press.

Schlesinger, A. (1992). *The disuniting of America*. New York: Norton.

Scholes, R. (1966). Narration and narrativity in film and fiction. In *Semiotics and interpretation* (pp. 68–83). New Haven, CT: Yale University Press.

Scholes, R. (1968). *Elements of fiction*. New York: Oxford University Press.

Scholes, R., & Kellogg, R. (1966). *The nature of narrative*. New York: Oxford University Press.

Schudson, M. (1978a). *Discovering the news: A social history of American newspapers*. New York: Basic Books.

Schudson, M. (1978b). The ideal of conversation in the study of mass media. *Communication Research, 5*, 320–329.

Schumacher, E. F. (1977). *A guide for the perplexed*. New York: Harper & Row.

Senge, P. M. (1990). *The fifth discipline: The art and practice of the learning organization*. New York: Doubleday.

Shannon, C., & Weaver, W. (1949). *The mathematical theory of communication*. Champaign-Urbana: University of Illinois Press.

Shaw, D. (1993, March 31). Trust in media on decline. *Los Angeles Times*, pp. A1, A16–18.

Shepherd, L. (1973). *The history of street literature*. London: David & Charles, Newton Abbot.

Sims, N. (Ed.). (1984). *The literary journalists*. New York: Ballantine.

Snyder, G. (1990). *The practice of the wild*. San Francisco: North Point Press.

Snyder, L. L., & Morris, R. B. (Eds.). (1942). *A treasury of great reporting*. New York: Simon & Schuster.

Stamets, R. S. (1988, April 23). A desolate area of Kenya has one product: Children. *St. Petersburg Times*, p. 1A.

Stein, M. L. (1992, November 28). Here we go again! *Editor & Publisher*, p. 11.

Stephens, M. (1988). *History of news: From the drum to the satellite*. New York: Viking.

Stephenson, W. (1964). The ludenic theory of newsreading. *Journalism Quarterly, 41*, 367–374.

Stephenson, W. (1967). *The play theory of mass communication*. Chicago: University of Chicago Press.

Stewart, J. (1978). Foundations of dialogic communication. *Quarterly Journal of Speech, 64*, 183–201.

Stewart, J. (1989). *Bridges not walls* (5th ed.). New York: McGraw-Hill.

Suzuki, D., & Knudtson, P. (1992). *Wisdom of the elders*. New York: Bantam Books.

Tannen, D. (1989). *Talking voices: Repetition, dialogue, and imagery in conversational discourse*. Cambridge: Cambridge University Press.

Tannen, D. (1990). *You just don't understand: Women and men in conversation*. New York: William Morrow.

Taylor, C. (1991). The dialogical self. In D. R. Hiley, J. F. Bohman, & R. Shusterman (Eds.), *The interpretive turn: Philosophy, science, culture* (pp. 304–314). Ithaca, NY: Cornell University Press.

Tedlock, D. (1983). *The spoken word and the work of interpretation*. Philadelphia: University of Pennsylvania Press.

Terkel, S. (1992). *Race: How blacks and whites think and feel about the American obsession*. New York: New Press.

"Time" goes on-line, interactive, this fall. (1993, July 26). *USA Today*, p. 2B.

Tinder, G. (1980). *Community: Reflections on a tragic ideal*. Baton Rouge: Louisiana State University Press.

Tomas, L. (1992, October 16). Phrase was damaging to American Indians. *St. Petersburg Times*, p. 2.

Tuchman, G. (1972). Objectivity as strategic ritual: An examination of newsmen's notions of objectivity. *American Journal of Sociology, 77*, 660–670.

Tuchman, G. (1978). *Making news: A study in the construction of reality*. New York: Free Press.

United States v. Associated Press. (1943). 52 F.Supp. 362 (S.D.N.Y. 1943).

van Dijk, T. A. (1988). *News as discourse*. Hillsdale, NJ: Lawrence Erlbaum.

Warner, W. L. (1959). *The living and the dead*. New Haven, CT: Yale University Press.

Warner, W. L. (1976). Mass media: The transformation of a political hero. In J. E. Combs & M. W. Mansfield (Eds.), *Drama in life: The uses of communication in society* (pp. 200–211). New York: Hastings House.

Weaver, D. H. (1991). *The American journalist* (2nd ed.). Bloomington: Indiana University Press.

West, C. (1992, August 2). Talk of race. *New York Times*, Sec. VI, pp. 24, 25.

White, D. M. (1964). The gatekeeper: A case study in the selection of news. In L. A. Dexter & D. M. White (Eds.), *People, society and mass communications* (pp. 160–172). New York: Free Press.

White, H. (1980). The value of narrativity in the representation of reality. In W.J.T. Mitchell (Ed.), *On narrative* (pp. 8–24). Chicago: University of Chicago Press.

Wiener, N. (1967). *The human use of human beings: Cybernetics and society.* New York: Avon.

Wolfe, T. (1973). *The new journalism.* New York: Harper & Row.

Wolvin, A., & Coakley, C. (1991). *Listening* (4th ed.). Dubuque, IA: William C. Brown.

Wong, W. (1991, May 10). Anti-pc people way off key. *Oakland Tribune*, p. C15.

Woo, W. F. (1991, November 10). Journalists risk becoming disconnected. *St. Louis Post-Dispatch*, p. B1.

Woo, W. F. (1992, April 19). Understanding our neighbors. *St. Louis Post-Dispatch*, p. B1.

Wurman, R. S. (1990). *Information anxiety: What to do when information doesn't tell you what you need to know.* New York: Bantam Books.

Zarefsky, D. (1992). Spectator politics and the revival of public argument. *Communication Monographs, 59*, 411–414.

Index

About the Authors

ROB ANDERSON is Professor and Director of Graduate Studies in the Department of Communication at Saint Louis University. He is the author of *Students as Real People: Interpersonal Communication and Education* (1979); co-author of *Before the Story: Interviewing and Communication Skills for Journalists* (1989), *Questions of Communication: A Practical Introduction to Theory* (1993), and *Accounting and Communication* (forthcoming); and co-editor of *The Reach of Dialogue: Confirmation, Voice, and Community* (forthcoming).

ROBERT DARDENNE is Associate Professor at the School of Mass Communications at the University of South Florida at St. Petersburg. He has also had a distinguished career as an investigative reporter, writer, and editor in New York, Washington, D.C., Louisiana, and Mexico City. His writing has appeared in the *Journal of American Culture* and in *Media, Myth and Narratives*, edited by James Carey (1988).

GEORGE M. KILLENBERG is Professor in the School of Mass Communications at the University of South Florida at St. Petersburg. He is the author of *Public Affairs Reporting: Covering the News in the Information Age* (1992), and co-author, with Rob Anderson, of *Before the Story: Interviewing and Communication Skills for Journalists* (1989).